LEATHERWORK

Also in The Crafts Series from Little, Brown
Gerald Clow, General Editor

BLACK AND WHITE PHOTOGRAPHY
Henry Horenstein

POTTERY
Cora Pucci

WOODWORK
Raphael Teller

CROCHET
Mary Tibbals Ventre

Forthcoming

STAINED GLASS
Barbara Frazier and
Gerry Clow

WEAVING
Elfleda Russell

LEATHERWORK
A Basic Manual

BENJAMIN MALESON

LITTLE, BROWN AND COMPANY — BOSTON — TORONTO

First Edition

T10/74

The drawings in this book are by the author and his brother, Joseph Maleson.

LIBRARY OF CONGRESS CATALOGING IN PUBLICATION DATA
Maleson, Benjamin.
    Leatherwork; a basic manual.

    (Little, Brown crafts series)
    Bibliography: p.
    1. Leather work.   I. Title.
TT290.M28   745.53'1   74-11079
ISBN 0-316-54457-5
ISBN 0-316-54450-7 (pbk.)

Published simultaneously in Canada by Little, Brown & Company (Canada) Limited
Printed in the United States of America

This book is dedicated to my mother, whose instruction and perfectionism guided me in my early work, to Jacob Siegel who encouraged my understanding of leather, to those who have worked and shared the free flow of ideas with me, and to all craftspeople whose works fill our daily lives with beauty.

The Little, Brown Craft Series is designed and published for the express purpose of giving the beginner — usually a person trained to use his head, not his hands — an idea of the basic techniques involved in a craft, as well as an understanding of the inner essence of that medium. Authors were sought who do not necessarily have a "name" but who thoroughly enjoy sharing their craft, and all their sensitivities to its unique nature, with the beginner. Their knowledge of their craft is vital, although it was realized from the start that one person can never teach all the techniques available.

The series helps the beginner gain a sense of the spirit of the craft he chooses to explore, and gives him enough basic instruction to get him started. Emphasis is laid on creativity, as crafts today are freed from having to be functional; on process, rather than product, for in the making is the finding; and on human help, as well as technical help, as so many prior teaching tools have said only "how" and not "why." Finally, the authors have closed their books with as much information on "next steps" as they could lay their hands on, so that the beginner can continue to learn about the craft he or she has begun.

GERALD CLOW

Workshop designing can never be a prosperous way of life and will always be extremely hard work. Against this, the experience will be educative, good work can be done, and a small living well-earned.

Norman Potter,
What Is a Designer:
Education and Practice

Contents

Acknowledgments

I began writing this book at the enthusiastic urging of Gerry Clow. Gerry and I met while he was editor of the crafts column for the *Boston Globe*. He has transcended the role of literary agent with his genuine warmth and friendship. Because of this I will forget that his encouragement took me away from creative craftwork for close to a year, while I learned how to compose a book and use a typewriter. The typewriter belonged to my brother, Joseph Maleson, who also did the artwork for the book. Much more than this, he selflessly shared his home with me through many exhausting months while we worked together. Much of this book was written and composed on index cards, a gift from my father who has written his own book in this way. In addition he provided me with a studio and a reserved amount of thoughtful criticism. His assistance has been invaluable. Many thanks to Ira Silverman for his valuable information about leather skins.

Robert Blacker and Peter Colton did the fine photography. They endured many difficult sessions with me. I will always value their friendship.

Parts of the first manuscript were typed by my dear friend Dinny Myerson, who shared her life with me during the years that we worked at the Laughing Alley crafts co-op. Dinny's loving spirit, ever present in her simple pottery, has been infinitely inspiring to me.

To all my fellow leatherworkers and to all the craftspeople who have shown me such extraordinary friendship, I extend my own friendship and grateful appreciation.

Finally, I wish to thank my editors, Dick McDonough and Leslie Arnold. I am especially indebted to Leslie, whose patient, constructive editing changed the numerous awkward spots into clear, readable material, and who generously retyped the final manuscript.

Introduction

Any library has several books on leatherwork which will tell you how to do fancy leather lacing and leather carving. These are almost all vintage books which have nothing to say about the environment that leads people to create with their hands items of value to them and those around them. They ignore the artist's life-style and seem to focus on that section of our population which can only treat the craft in an uninvolved way. Patterns for billfolds and purses occupy many of the pages of these books and creative design seems to be discouraged. This must have filled a need at one time, but now with crafts becoming an important life-style, more needs to be said. For five years I have grown with the crafts movement within my own sphere of leatherworking. I have learned many of the problems as well as the finer points of living the craft. I hope that my suggestions will help those who are only casually interested as well as those planning to involve themselves completely, as I did.

My Design Concepts and Philosophy

Why do leatherwork? Too often in this culture run by big money and politics we find ourselves living someone else's concept of what we should be. There are times when each of us feels the need to reassert our relationship with those materials that make up our lives. For many, working with these materials can serve as a beneficial release from the pressures and complexities of our overmechanized society. Crafts of all varieties are becoming an important part of the lives of aware young people. Crafts allow those who are dissatisfied to escape from the system and realize their own lives. By being designers we can create our own environments, drawing on our most intimate influences to express our concepts of ourselves in our self-made surroundings. Although the techniques I will show you are for leather only, I believe that from the point of view of the designer all crafts are interrelated. Thus craftspeople who develop interdisciplinary skills will better be able to control their environment. A knowledge of metalworking techniques coupled with facilities for doing metalwork, for instance, enables you to create your own hardware: buckles, buttons, and the like. Such hardware enhances your leatherwork by making it a more personal statement. More advanced metalworking skills would allow you to make your own tools and equipment, further developing your ability to control your environment.

Leatherworking is not merely a pastime or profession, it is

a life-style. Leatherworkers need not live in the back room of their workshops to participate in this life-style (although they surely can). No, we need only to be attuned to the importance of a balanced environment and a unified family of men and women throughout the world, for it is from this environment that we take our materials and inspiration, and from our brothers and sisters that we learn how to share our spirits and our visions.

There is a phenomenon among leatherworkers which I call the leatherworkers school, in which each leatherworker freely teaches and in turn learns from his colleagues. At the same time each leatherworker is continually developing and improving new techniques. The leatherworkers who keep their techniques secret are rare; they are known as "stingy buggers."

After making my first pair of sandals I was dissatisfied, so I went to a number of leather shops to see how others had dealt with the problems that I had experienced. From watching Nick Newman working at his shop, Leather Design of Harvard Square, I gained a great deal of insight. When I finished my second pair of sandals I showed them to Nick and, after he commented about the possibility of my going into competition across the street, he made suggestions about changing the strap arrangement to provide better support for the foot and keep the sandal from twisting. However cynical Nick may have been, he gave me good advice; the design I ended up with on my third pair has become my most popular style.

When I first decided to make shoes for myself I was looking at a pair of boots made by Tom Tisdell from the Tisdell Sandal Shop in Cambridge, Massachusetts. They had a rugged look that a lumberjack would love, yet a graceful line that showed the love that created them. Tom explained the important foot measurements to me: the length, first joint, waist, and around the heel. He also explained his method for making a pattern. Then he told me the basic principles of lasting the boot, naming each part of the boot construction as he showed it to me.

These two instances were by no means unique; they are

only individual examples of the abundant freedom with which leatherworkers share their ideas.

The leather district in Boston is two blocks long, with additional shops and offices on the side streets. Most of the places are tannery representatives which deal to large manufacturers such as shoe factories. Only a few shops sell to individual craftsmen. Most of these are jobbers; they buy manufacturers' overstock as well as regular tannery stock. One such shop is the M. Siegel Company, run by Jacob and Harold Siegel. Jacob and Harold Siegel are individuals who have a genuine feeling for the special qualities in each type of leather. Jacob has never hesitated to go out of his way to explain what gives various leathers their particular qualities or to show me unusual pieces of leather. His enthusiasm has inspired me throughout my experience with leather.

There are four components to a professional leather studio: work tables, tools and machines, expendable supplies such as leather and dyes, and displays of original work. My first workshop, though quite simple, served me well for almost three years. My table was a large oak desk that I picked up at an auction for two dollars. I had a small Neolite cutting board, a knife, three bevelers, a ruler and an old cobbler's sewing machine. I made eight styles of handbags, innumerable belts, and fifty to a hundred pairs of sandals each summer. I displayed my work by wearing items that I made. I either took orders or sold the items right off my back to people who admired my work. When I started selling sandals, I made a pair for each member of my family, and with the four or five styles thus assembled my customers could get a good starting idea of what they wanted. As I developed more designs, I made drawings and took photographs in order to have visual descriptions of each style.

My ideas about design developed naturally as I grew familiar with the leather. My first impressions of leather were actually of its odor and supple character. Later, as I became more aware of the variety of textures uniquely belonging to leather, I began to enjoy adding color to these unique textures. At first I chose shades and tones of brown, as I felt that

they were the most "natural." It was a while before I would admit that leather had a right to be colored purple, or red, or green, but in time I grew fascinated by the entire range of colors available.

Subtle shifts of color and shade are what make leather look so rich. The same principle of subtle shifts makes sunsets spectacular, mountains breathtaking, and spring forests and deep pools of water soul-satisfying. Leather articles are enhanced when different areas are shaded differently. The variance in absorption of dyes by leather helps to achieve this effect. As skill is developed in the use of leather dyes and finishes, this aspect of design can be controlled precisely.

Each type of leather has its own characteristic texture. Ability to control the textural aspect of design, then, lies in the familiarity with all the various types of leather. The texture of vegetable-tanned leathers can also be altered while damp by the use of modeling tools and stamps. Innumerable patterns are possible, allowing great freedom of personal expression.

Construction is also an important aspect of design. The method of putting an object together can be the focal point of the piece, it can be relatively inconspicuous, or it can blend simply and harmoniously with the overall design. The choice of machine or hand stitching, or lacing, or gluing, or the use of various types of hardware creates a wide range of possibilities for project construction as an element of design.

Form is one of the most important elements of creative design. It is humbling to think of the infinite numbers of refined forms that exist in nature. Because of this, our inspiration most often comes from natural forms. Frequently we find that artistic interpretation of a natural form leads to the most pleasing designs. We can also gain inspiration from the contemporary and traditional forms of other crafts. A day spent studying these forms, either in nature, in museums or in the showrooms of contemporary craftsmen, is never wasted.

Decorative units or motifs may be applied to leather by stamping and tooling, burning, appliqués, silhouette and inlays as well as with stitching, lacing, and hardware. Component

eather swing made from heavy sole leather, vith braided elkhide ropes secured by vide tabs of French-back cowhide

parts should blend harmoniously and irrelevant material should be eliminated. One should never use any decorative design in a way that would obscure the beauty of the leather itself. Decorations should enhance the surfaces that they are applied to.

A good craftsperson must always consider function as a major consideration of the design. Stress should be eliminated as much as possible, and movements and mechanisms should work easily. Good functional design can rarely be spontaneous. More often it is influenced by the designs of other craftsmen and is achieved through patient experimentation in order to improve upon those designs. While experimenting with a design, many mistakes are bound to happen. There is hardly a mistake that cannot be corrected in a pleasing manner. When you have modified a design so that all the parts work and when it becomes a refined projection of the function, then you will be proud of your work and the people who use it will be served well. If you elaborate on your successful designs and add artistic decoration, people will notice your work and your fame will spread.

No design, however artistic, can make up for poor workmanship. I want to stress the importance of continually striving for the highest standards of quality in all you make, although I know that this goal is sometimes impractical and unprofitable. In the long run, however, the satisfaction of fine craftsmanship is its own reward, much more valuable than the monetary payment of the customer.

Simple designs without elaborate ornamentation are often the best for displaying your skill as a craftsperson. Simplification rather than elaboration is the path to practical design.

Elaborations are made to obscure flaws and mistakes, to satisfy capricious impulses, or as acts of love. Flaws and mistakes require a great deal of work to correct, but the results can be extremely rewarding if they are approached as a challenge for the designer. Capricious elaborations are unprofitable unless you have wealthy customers willing to pay for such caprice, but they can be eminently satisfying. Acts of love speak for themselves — no other reward is necessary.

bbled hatbox made from nine different thers. Inner collar fastened to support th a continuous strip of rolled cowhide, otted at each fastening point. "Arizona" hat ade from 1½-ounce chrome-tanned cow-de with grosgrain binding to hold brim ape. Neck strap attached to sweatband

I want to teach you how to *learn* to be a leatherworker. To a certain extent I am forced to compromise my teaching methods by showing you technical procedures. Leatherwork as I know it, however, is an intuitive process that develops into an intimate relationship. This is a relationship in which each side constantly tests the limits of the other, and each test is educational. This is true of any craft. The lesson of a single mistake is more valuable than any I could teach here. The beauty of a sunrise in the mountains cannot be told in words — it must be experienced. Of course the sun must also rise on rotten days, otherwise we would not appreciate its magnificence when it rises in glory. Some mistakes cannot be corrected with even the greatest effort. These allow us to see the glory of mistakes which lead to original, creative, and artistic solutions. I cannot describe the education I have received from my mistakes. I can only encourage you to use your mistakes as tests. Tackle each problem with love and patience — these are the roots of creativity. Never be afraid to create new problems, to search for new aspects of the material with which to express yourself. Always be patient. The more time you put into a design the more elegant the result will be. Whether you search for form, or texture, or strength, or color, or humor, or function, search with love and the material itself will teach you.

Peltry

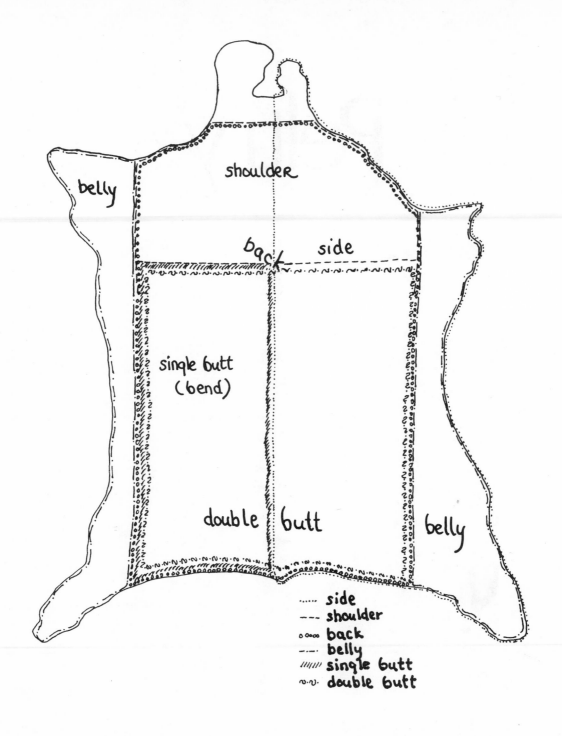

belly

shoulder

belly

back · side

single butt
(bend)

double butt

belly

...... side
— — — shoulder
o ooo back
— · — belly
///// single butt
ᴨ·ᴨ double butt

This section is concerned with the material upon which the art is based — animal skins. Without them the craft of leatherworking could not exist. When primitive man first wrapped himself in the skins of the animals that he had killed for food or in self-defense, he began the most ancient of crafts. At that time resources were abundant. He would not have believed that the supply of animal skins would someday be limited. But today, through the careless use of our animal resources, we have eliminated many valuable animals, part of whose value was in their skins. A list of endangered species from the U.S. Department of the Interior, Fish and Wildlife Service, includes over three hundred animal species in danger of extinction. Over one hundred species and subspecies on this list are from the United States alone. Skins and other products manufactured from these animals must be boycotted, as this is the only way to stop the slaughter. Whales, seals, kangaroos, wildcats, alligators, crocodiles, boas, the timber wolf, the red wolf, many kinds of deer (only the key deer and Columbian white-tailed deer in this country), gazelles, and antelopes (only the Sonoran Pronghorn antelope in this country) are threatened by poachers as well as by loss of habitat, and it is up to the consumers to eliminate the market which supports these illegal hunting activities.

Leatherwork can, however, be an ecological craft, since it can use an important by-product of the meat industry. This includes skins of cows, horses, sheep, goats, and pigs. Many kinds of deerskins and elkskins may also be used with a free conscience, as deer and elk populations must be controlled in any event to prevent overcompetition for food, which can result in herd starvation. The joy of leatherworking lies in finding the perfect leather and then finding the perfect use for it. When the leather is right and the project is right you will know it in the tips of your fingers, and anything you make from it will come out right.

A man who loved his Alfa Romeo asked me to put together a leather interior — seat covers, door panels, the works. Apparently he considered price more important than skill (although the price I quoted him was low according to the automobile seat cover industry), for he ended up commissioning a novice who had worked exclusively on ready-made sandals. He used some very soft, beautiful glove-tanned calfskin for the job. It was only a short time before the seats were all bagged out from the stress of being sat upon. The result was atrocious. If he had used a firmer leather it might have been superb. The leather chosen must be suited to the specific use for which it is intended. You can't make a wallet from sole leather, nor can you make sandals from kidskin.

People coming into my shop often ask, "How did you learn all this?" My fingers taught me, and it is time for your fingers to get behind the rest of your hand and put it to work. You will never learn anything from this book that will make you a good leatherworker unless your fingers understand what I am saying, and they will have to try it themselves. "Learning," says my swami, "is nothing more than realizing that you already knew something that you already knew." Before reading this section, go to a leather shop if you can and touch every piece of leather there. I always buy leather by touch as well as by color, weight, and type. Touching is the only definite way to select leather.

A knowledge of leather is threefold. First, you should know what kind of animal the skin came from. Next, you should know how the skin was made into leather. Finally, you must learn how to use it so that it means something when you are done with it. A knowledge of leather is mostly guesswork, as my index card states so plainly.

What kinds of animals do skins come from? Dead animals. Vertebrates — fish, reptiles, amphibians, birds, and mammals. Fish and reptile skins both have scales. Mr. Siegel has some really unusual skins hanging in his office. Every time he comes across a rare skin he likes to stump me by making me guess what it's from. When he showed me the dyed codfish skins I thought that they were just some kind of snakeskin because of the scales. But I was wrong. Fish skins are heavier and stiffer than snakeskins. Snakeskins are very thin and have practically no flesh under the scales. Snakeskins are often dyed bright colors to enhance the decorative possibilities inherent in their scaly surfaces. These codfish skins were similarly dyed, bright blue and yellow. Mr. Siegel then showed me a South American frogskin; naturally it was dyed green. I had never heard of frogskins being tanned or seen a frog that big so I thought it must be some sort of lizard. Wrong again.

I have mentioned three categories of skins: fish, reptile, and amphibian. Bird skins are not sold in any leather shops that I know of, but are widely available from sporting supply houses that carry materials for making trout flies. They often put out comprehensive catalogs describing the different kinds of loose feathers, breasts, backs, tails and wings.

Snake, lizard, frog, fish, and bird skins all fit in the classification "novelty leathers." Generally they are thin, fragile and not very soft — clearly not suitable for areas of stress or abrasion. Instead, they are used for their decorative quality.

I have also experimented successfully with vegetarian leatherwork. The hides of many fruits can be dried and used in many ways: as containers, lids, or purely for decoration. Nuts, seeds, and pits can be put to various uses as buttons, knobs, beads, and the like. Gourds, leaves, bark, grasses, bamboo and other plant materials can all be fashioned into serviceable articles. While such vegetarian leatherwork is often impractical by itself, it can be very useful when done in conjunction with your standard leatherwork. Besides eliminating a part of your waste, it can lead to many interesting designs.

Cowhide is the most commonly used of all the mammal skins. It is strong, it comes in conveniently large hides, and it is available in a variety of different forms. It can be made soft or very hard. It can be firm or supple, thick or thin, spongy or compressed, oily, waxy or dry. The flesh is made up of long fibers in comparison with other leathers, and these fibers can be brushed up into a beautiful soft nap. Cowhides are thick enough to be sliced in layers to form splits which can be made into the finest nappy suedes, or into rough shoe-grade suede. When the hides are vegetable-tanned, the leather is easily molded and the smooth surface, or "grain," can be impressed with tools after wetting. Hides tanned with metallic salts (i.e., chrome-tanned) remain less affected by water, and are often quite soft and supple. Cowhides are so large that they are usually divided into sections rather than sold in full hides. Full hides run anywhere from about thirty to sixty square feet. The divisions are standard. Half hides divided at the back-bone are called sides. Sides run from 13 to 28 square feet, the usual size being around 20 square feet. There are soft chrome-tanned garment sides about 2 to 3 ounces in thickness (in leather an ounce is approximately 1/64 inch); heavier bag leathers measuring 4 to 5 ounces, either chrome- or vegetable-tanned; 5-to-6-ounce latigo sides, a waxy leather used for straps, laces, footwear, bags, etc.; and heavier latigo up to 9 or 10 ounces for belts, straps, and the popular tooled, laced bags. The round, iron frame chair shown here is made of 8-ounce latigo. Latigo is characteristically a yellow or yellowish tan color, but is also made in natural (a sort of grayish cream color), cherry and brown. The waxy fatliquoring (a lubricating process) gives latigo a rich patina and acts as a *mild* resist to any colorants applied to the leather. Actually, if the leather is too waxy it is hard to dye evenly. The best latigo has just enough fatliquoring to make it respond well to dyes and still be fairly supple.

Vegetable-tanned sides traditionally come from England, so they are called English bag leather or English sides or, when they are from large calves, English kips. Kips run from about 6 to 12 feet. Vegetable-tanned leather is also referred to as

Hand-stitched iron frame chair made latigo cowhide. Cobbled briefcase ma of cowhide shoulder. Folding chair made chrome-oil-tanned cowhide with latigo l

"oak" because of the use of oak bark as a tanning agent.

The next large subdivision commonly used is the back. This is the portion of the hide running the length of the backbone and extending 2 to 3 feet on either side (making it 4 to 6 feet wide). Basically, it is a hide with the bellies cut off. This makes it more uniform, as the bellies are the most mushy and uneven part of the hide. I have seen backs as small as 12 feet and as large as 38 feet. Backs are very good for economical cuttings because the edges are almost perfectly straight. They are always vegetable-tanned (there must be exceptions but I haven't seen them). The best backs come from France and England with a fine, smooth, even grain and measure about 6 to 9 ounces. Those from England are well curried and have a waxy feel. These are the beautiful "English bridle backs." They are cut on the backbone, giving them the form of long narrow rectangles. English bridle leather commands high respect and high prices. It is superb belt leather. I have even used English bridle leather for sandal topsoles with excellent results. French backs, in comparison, are relatively dry and are full, or double, backs. This is wonderful leather for molding and modeling. It is very responsive when wet and takes a beautiful finish. Because the back has a tight fiber structure, this leather bevels cleanly and the edges burnish well. French backs are being used a great deal for cobbled bags in this area (the East Coast's answer to laced latigo bags).

The double butt is the portion from the tail to about the middle of the hide, with the soft edges trimmed off. This section, like the back, is very uniform in thickness. The butt is the heaviest part of the hide and is the part used for soling leather. For this purpose it is made into "bends." A bend is a single butt, the same as a double butt, divided along the backbone. Bends are made from the full thickness of the hide and would be difficult to manage as full double butts. Double butts are roughly about 4 feet square. As you can imagine, this is a very convenient size and shape. Four-foot straps are just about the perfect size for belt straps. There is very little waste when a double butt is made into belts.

Double butts are generally split into about 7-to-13-ounce

thicknesses. They are made in vegetable, chrome and oil-chrome tannages. Vegetable tanning is used for domestic and Spanish double butts, and of course oak bends. The domestic and Spanish double butts are similar to the backs, but the grain is a bit coarser and the skins heavier. The Spanish is the finer of the two; it really comes close to the French backs, but it isn't quite as mellow. Chrome double butts are softer and stronger. The chrome tannage makes this leather very hard to cut; even though it is fairly soft, it dulls blades very quickly. It is popular for straps on ready-made sandals because of its strength and because it is made in vat-dyed colors so that only edge dyeing is required. Its tendency to stretch is a drawback. Because the fibers are fluffed up in the softening process it is hard to bevel neatly, and the edges do not burnish well. It is useful, but it isn't really beautiful. The oil-chrome double butt is the most supple leather of its weight range. It is available from about 8 ounces to a very thick 13 ounces. It is very expensive but wonderful stuff. This is the leather that the famous Walter Dyer moccasin is made from and the leather I used when I was commissioned to make "one heavy-duty shock-absorbent leather case for Ferruzine 10,000 X micro sync. battery inverter." This leather makes great braided belts that turn brass buckles a purplish color. To compensate for the stretching I start with a loose braid and tighten the braid as the belt stretches. The color change just happens and can't be avoided.

A bit more about bends. The most common are the oak bends. They are sold by weight, and average about 12 pounds. They are practically all the same size, so the difference in weight corresponds to the thickness of the leather. Thickness is measured by "irons" in bends, rather than by ounces. Oak bends are available in smaller, more select pieces, known as finders' bends. These are good for two to three pairs of soles. Shoe findings shops carry these as well as one-pair pieces and single-cut soles. They are more expensive, but they are graded carefully so that you can get absolutely consistent quality and weight if you choose to buy these select cuts.

Besides oak bends, you can get oiled and hydraulic oiled bends, chrome and snuff grain chrome bends, and stretched bends. Oiled and chrome bends are stronger and more resistant to abrasion, but they are not suitable for molding. Stretched bends are beautiful, very expensive, and hard to get, but they are worth it. Stretched bends mold fairly easily and hold an arch exceptionally well. The currying which is done to the leather when making these stretched bends produces a strong, flexible, resilient, durable topsole leather with a beautiful grain — a joy to work with. I also once bought a heavy, well-curried bend from Mr. Siegel, the like of which I have never seen since. A tanner's sample, it was very heavy and very supple with a beautiful feel, and it cut like butter. It was one of a kind and I used it very carefully. Finding a piece of leather like that is a thrilling, soul-satisfying experience for anyone who really loves this material.

The shoulder is the section of the back that is left after cutting off the double butt. It is a very popular cut for belts as it is an easy size to handle, both physically and monetarily. Shoulders average about eight to ten feet. This is one of the less expensive cuts, primarily because of the prominent fat wrinkles. The fat wrinkles don't necessarily detract from the beauty of the leather. In fact, there is a definite appeal to these natural markings. The shoulders are generally oak-tanned and are often treated rather heavily with oil. Care must be taken not to allow oiled shoulders to come into contact with other leather, as the oil tends to bleed. Shoulders are available in a range of thicknesses, from 5 to 6 ounces to 9 to 10 ounces. The first full cut of leather that I ever bought was a heavily oiled "teak" shoulder. It is interesting to note two things here. First of all, the price of a cut of leather seems to correspond, at least a little, to the price of a cut of meat from the same part of the animal; second, leather is often given the name of a wood it resembles in color, thus the names "teak," "chestnut," "mahogany," "cherry," "maple," and even "oak," although the latter also refers to the tanning process itself. We also see names like "saddle," "honey," "cream," as well as "natural" and all of the primary colors.

The bellies are the least uniform, most irregular in shape, and least expensive parts of the hide. They are generally made up in belt weight and are oak-tanned. Bellies are economical for small articles of this weight and for areas where appearance is not crucial, such as innersoles for shoes.

Range markings such as scratches, tick marks, and brands occur occasionally. As long as these wounds are healed they needn't be avoided. Hides with such imperfections are often sorted out as lower grades and sold at a lower cost than perfectly clean skins. When I use leather with prominent range markings, I like to let the design of the piece be influenced by the patterns of the markings. Large unhealed scratches, wounds and brands must be considered waste since they weaken the leather considerably. Leather with overly consistent grain markings or without any markings whatsoever must be viewed suspiciously as an attempt to make clean skins out of ones with many imperfections. This is done by buffing off all the surface grain along with the undesirable markings, applying some sort of smooth finish, and then "plating" or "embossing" the hides in huge presses. Plated hides are smooth and embossed hides are textured. I feel this destroys the beauty of the leather. Such corrected grain hides are laboratory products reflecting none of the natural beauty of full grain leather, and as such they should be avoided. Of course there are very clean skins of full grain cowhide and it is a pleasure to come across them, but they are not very common and may be prohibitively expensive.

In contrast to cowhides, calfskins are generally very clean, with a neat, tiny, even grain that is very smooth. Calfskins generally measure from 4 to 12 feet with a weight of around 1 to 4 ounces. Calf is usually chrome-tanned to a firm consistency. The close, tight grain naturally makes it a bit stiffer than the open, loose grain of mature cowhides of the same weight.

There are a number of processes used to soften calfskin to create different consistencies. Boarded or box calf is created by putting the skins through a machine which imparts a box-like pattern to the leather. The leather is folded back on itself and rolled between cork-covered boards and rollers. Box calf is simply boarded calf that has been rolled in two directions, the second perpendicular to the first. Calfskins treated in this manner become more supple while retaining much of their original firmness. This is obviously a highly directional type of softening; the resulting leather is good for making mellow wallets, cases, bags and fancy belts and shoes. Box calf is nice pleasant leather.

Staking is a sort of stretching and flexing process which is used to soften leather. The staking machine grabs the leather in its jaws and pulls on it rather violently. The skin is held and turned by the staking machine operator. Imagine you have a skin held taut on a frame and you are working the leather with both hands — one in a cupped shape on top of the skin and the other clenched in a fist underneath the skin — the two hands fitting together with the leather in between, pulling and stretching in all directions. The ancient process from which the name derived simply involved pulling the skin over a stake set in the ground until it attained the desired softness.

The amount of lubrication in the fibers also affects the softness of the leather. Leather is lubricated by fatliquoring. The fatliquors are mostly oils which are applied in an emulsified state to aid penetration and insure even distribution throughout the fibers. The oils are from either petroleum bases or animal fats. Egg yolks and lanolin are sometimes used, but basically they're tallow, fish oils, and mineral oils.

Another softening technique that comes to mind is tumbling. Jacob Siegel explained tumble-tanned leather to me shortly after I first met him. I had picked out an extremely soft side of bag leather which he said had been tumbled soft. "It's really a very simple process. They put the skins into huge drums (sort of like oversized clothes dryers) and keep them turning until the leather is nice and soft."

Really great leather comes from goats. Goatskin is extremely strong. Lace made of goatskin is stronger than lace cut from cowhide, elk or deer. I keep my keys on a lace $\frac{1}{16}$ inch wide cut from 1-ounce goatskin. There is nothing else like it. Goat is usually quite soft and stretchy. It makes wonderful trousers, but the knees and seat must be lined to keep them from bagging. Prestretching helps minimize distortion after a garment is put together. My esteemed leatherworking friend Jim Earle, who is a genuine craftsman, prestretches goat and deerskins by clipping weights around the edges and hanging them for several days or weeks. A similar process known as toggling is used commercially in which the skins are clamped to stretchers and then exposed to heat in order to shrink them. Thus both excessive stretch and shrinkage are controlled. Goatskin is characterized by an unmistakable extremely large grain. This graininess gives the leather a beautiful effect when it is colored with a transparent dye (like Fiebing's Antique Dye), which highlights the raised surfaces of the grain while sinking into and darkening the recessed areas.

Kidskins are taken from very young animals, so the grain is much more compact than in older goatskins, but they still have a heavier grain than the skins of most other young animals. However, I have used tiny, unborn kidskins with fine, smooth graining. These kidskins were only about a half ounce in thickness, and the footages (about 1 to 1½ feet) were marked in the center of a stamp proclaiming that these skins were a product of Mexico. I use this leather for lining wallets. Jim Earle made it into full wallets (very compact). I also use it for covering and lining small cases, boxes, and similar items. Because it is so thin, it stretches easily around objects to be covered. Unfortunately for leatherworkers, unborn kidskins are very rare.

Ordinary kidskins are often made up into beautiful suedes because the flesh has such fine, close fibers. The coarser grades are used only for shoes, but when the nap is brushed up all the way it earns the name "silk suede." Kidskins are generally between three and four and a half feet, which limits their uses. I find them perfect for vests. A four-panel vest complete with pockets, buttonholes and facings requires about 12 to 14 feet of kidskin, or about four skins. This gives me a few usable scraps which I like to make into linings, inserts, pockets, buttonholes and the like. In short, any small application which would be unnoticed by itself can turn into something special when made from this extraordinary stuff.

One other type of kid that I've had the chance to use is metallic-mylar-treated. I've seen it in an incredible platinum pink, sapphire blue, and that shade of green that you can see if you look between the blue and the orange in the evening sunset. It has an ultrafuturistic reflective surface, but its real beauty is that the mylar is thin enough to reveal the full grain of the leather. That's really amazing, not because the mylar is so thin, but because the finish was actually applied to the finest *full grain* kidskins. It could so easily have been a cover-up like so many other metallic leathers. Someone was proud of these skins for each one was stamped with a date. The platinum pink skins were dated August 9, 1954. Most people are unimpressed when they see this leather (many simply don't like it), but I assure you that it takes a lot of looking at leather to find anything this special.

You may never see some of the leather I talk about. J. W. Waterer is considered the top authority on leather today; in his book *Leather and Craftsmanship* (do read it) he mentions Russian reindeer leather, a very soft leather on which the grain has been "friezed" off, leaving a velvety nap. I have never seen any Russian reindeer leather. I hope I will recognize it when I do. Most of the leathers that I remember with pleasure have been one-shot deals — job lots that could not be reordered once they ran out. Job lots are usually manufacturers' surplus. They come from shoe and glove factories, tanneries, etc. These manufacturers want to make sure that they don't run short so they buy more material than they need. When they finish a production item, or if they discontinue it for one reason or another, they often end up with an excess. These surpluses are sold to jobbers at a loss, just to keep them from piling up. The jobber, then, can buy at below tanners' prices. Then he has to find a buyer. It may be you. Usually jobbers try to sell large lots of thousands of feet of leather, but most of them are friendly and glad to help you out if you are looking for something special. In recent years, more and more jobbers have started carrying regular lines of leather, almost to the exclusion of the job lots, in response to the great number of individuals interested in working with leather. At least in Boston, it's getting harder and harder to get special low-demand leathers. M. Siegel Company used to have a whole bin of beautiful two-to-three-ounce charcoal gray snuffed grain calf. This leather came from Germany, where the best calf in the world is made. It was fabulous for making my special top hats. Snuffing the grain (done with fine abrasives) creates an incredibly fine suede with a practically nonexistent nap. This is only possible on the grain side because the fibers of the grain are so dense. I once found the tanner's label between two skins in one of the bundles. It was a diamond-shaped piece of tissue paper printed backwards with silver ink "Cornelius Heyl — Worms" with two serpentine dragons in the center. Imagine it — the most subtly exquisite of suedes and the label must match; printed backwards, the silver ink has to be viewed *through* the tissue paper. I used small amounts of this leather, a few skins at a time, for a couple of years until the whole bin was sold to a manufacturer. It's sad to think that I can no longer get any of that snuffed calf, but I kept the label as a souvenir. That's the way it is with job-lot leathers; you may find something fantastic at a reasonable price, but you can't ever be sure how long it will last. I once got the most beautiful deerskin I have ever used for 50 cents a foot when the going price was $1.20 a foot by buying from a jobber, but if I had been making a shirt or a pair of pants there would never have been enough. So although you may get a bargain price, you pay in the amount of time that you have to spend looking through odd lots to find what you want. The advantage of regular lines of leather is that you can simply order what you want and be pretty certain of getting it, and if you run out you can get more. Another way to buy leather is direct from tanneries or from the sorters. If they are willing to deal with individuals you will probably get a bargain. Sorters grade skins according to the number of imperfections (tick marks, holes, salt damage, etc.), and often cut off major imperfections. I was once given a large bundle of these trimmings for nothing. This kind of deal is great if you can find a use for scraps.

By going to sorters and tanners, I have gotten some very unusual skins: A white German stagskin, 18 feet and about ¼ to ½ inch thick, very soft; South American pigskins ⅜ inch thick, complete with nipples; elk shoulders over an inch thick (too thick to go through the splitting machine). I have seen walrus, linx and iguana skins tacked on walls as prize possessions. It is fun to spend a day looking around a tanning town (this is probably not true for people who live in one). In general, though, I expect that you will be buying from the regular stock available from the leather retailer or jobber (who may be the same dealer). Most types of cowhide, except prohibitively expensive varieties, are normally stocked. This includes shoulders, backs, butts, sides, and kips in vegetable tannages; latigo and oil grain sides, oiled shoulders and chrome double butts; chrome-tanned garment and bag sides and garment splits. Deerskin, chamois, goat, elk and antelope, sheepskins, garment calf, and horse bellies are also often available.

Deerskin is the softest of any leather. It has a fluffy fiber structure that gives it excellent insulating qualities. At the same time it has about the best "breathing" ability of any leather. The grain is smooth and buttery, and the flesh can be brushed up to a soft velvety nap. Besides all this, it is wonderfully strong and even handles repeated warm machine washings without ill effect. (Don't machine dry deerskin! Heat shrinks, shrivels, and stiffens.) The terms "buckskin," "doeskin" and "stagskin" indicate gender, stag being the heaviest skin, buck and doeskin being the lightest. Deerskin splits have recently become popular as a cheaper grade having many of the qualities of the full grain skins. The splits are soft and supple with a nice nap. Unlike cowhide splits, they seem to be pretty strong. The widest strip that I can break with my bare hands is ¼ inch.

It is also important to remember that deerskin was the chief leather used by the American Indians. They used it with such artfulness, economy and integrity that it is worthwhile to go to any museum displaying American Indian relics for inspiration. While I was at the American Museum of Natural History in New York, doing just that, I went to its library and found some American Indian recipes for making deerskin. Basically, Indian deerskin is not tanned; it is *worked* soft. First, the hair is removed from the hide, either by cutting it off or loosening it with lye resulting from the following process. Wood ashes are sprinkled on, then rubbed in. Next the hide is moistened, rolled up and set aside until the hair begins to loosen. Then the hide is soaked for three to six days. When the skin is removed from the water it is placed over the graining log, a log from which the bark has been removed. It is stuck obliquely into the ground so that the upper end is about waist high. Bits of flesh, fat and sinew are scraped off with a flesher, which is a small hoelike blade. Then the skin is reversed and the hair and epidermis are removed with a beamer, a tool with a curved blunt blade often made of the shinbone of the deer. If the hair doesn't come out easily, it is treated to a second and sometimes third application of the wood ash. During the fleshing and beaming operations, care should be taken to keep the skin uniformly thick. After this is done the skin is twisted and flexed until it has been worked to a degree of softness. Then it is stretched almost drumtight onto a frame. A brain paste is made by splitting the skull, removing the brains, and dissolving them in warm or hot water by crushing them with the fingers until they have been worked into a fluid paste. This is to be spread on the hide — there must be enough to cover it. If the brains are too small, liver paste is combined with it. It is better to have too much than too little. Excess paste can be stored by mixing the paste with moss, drying it near a slow fire, and squeezing it into cakes which can be remoistened for use. The brain paste is then spread on the skin and worked in until the fibers are saturated. Then the hide is removed from the frame and rinsed by soaking and wringing repeatedly. Between wringing and soaking, the skin is stretched and pulled out in all directions. The skin becomes soft, pliable and white.

Smoking is done with rotten wood, corncobs or chips of oak or beech thrown on coals in the smoke pit. The skin is hung over the pit above the smoke, and the edges and holes are sewn so the smoke will be trapped and distributed evenly. It is watched closely and the skin is removed when it reaches the desired color, yellow, tan or brown. It is then folded, smoked sides together, for a few days to set the color. For cleaning and coloring, colored clays such as yellow ochre are rubbed in, then shaken out, and the skin brushed. The effect of brain paste is not totally understood, except that it acts as a nutrient.

At the same time I saw the recipe for deerskin, I found directions for making rawhide. They are basically the same as the first steps in making deerskin. Rawhide is neither tanned nor softened. It is made by soaking and dehairing skins, then scraping them to a uniform thickness. If the skins are very heavy (such as elk or moose), the hair must be loosened with ashes. The lye resulting from the ashes weakens the grain, so ashes should not be used unless necessary. After the skins are dehaired and scraped, stretch the skins very tightly on a frame and allow them to dry in a cool, shady place.

Rawhide is wonderful stuff. The degree to which it will stretch when wet is truly surprising. As it dries, it shrinks back to its original size. This characteristic makes rawhide useful for such things as drumheads and snowshoe lacings. The rawhide is put on wet and pulled tight by hand. As it dries it gets tighter and tighter. The Indians used to attach heads on stone axes by wrapping wet rawhide over the head and around the handle. When it dried it conformed perfectly to the tool and the head was held on very securely. Rawhide is also translucent, and because of this I have found that it makes nice lampshades. The antique ivory color of the light is very pleasing. Rawhide is used on sail palms because it is hard enough to resist puncturing when pushing needles.

Probably none of the uses I have described will prompt you to buy a side of rawhide. I feel that it is important enough to deserve an extra word of persuasion. If you are ever in a position to get some rawhide, do not hesitate; you are sure to find many unexpected and surprising uses for this versatile material.

Horsehide is a fine leather with a tight, regular grain. The finest belts, sandal straps, and knife strops, as well as many fine motorcycle jackets, are made from it. Garment horse is hard to find. I have never had an opportunity to use any. Most of the skins I have seen have been pretty poor. It's too bad; if clean skins were available, without too many holes, they would make beautiful garments. What I've seen is soft, smooth and strong, but as I said, with too many holes. This is probably due to the shortage of horsehides in this country. Most of the horsehides available now have to be imported from Belgium.

I have seen beautiful full hides of pony and sides of horsehide tanned with the hair on. The full hides usually have nice manes. Horsehide is also available in bellies and butts. Horse butts are completely different from cow butts. The horse butt is known as the "shell" because of its remarkably tight fiber structure. Also, its shape is unmistakably that of a horse's butt. The best strops are made from shell horsehide. "Cordovan" has changed its meaning many times. Originally it referred to a bright red, alum- and sumac-tanned sheep or goatskin from Cordova, Spain. Now the term is applied to shell horsehide finished in a reddish brown color. The complete background is given in all the historical leather books I have read.

Horse bellies are one of my favorite leathers. In my opinion they make the finest belts, straps and laces. The reason I am so attached to horse belly leather is that it provides me with the opportunity to become a currier, dressing it with nutrient oils and softening it with my fingers as it tests the strength in my arm. I consider this the most intimate encounter I can have with leather. I can feel the fibers as they are transformed from a rigid state to a supple, flowing consistency. The flesh side of horsehide is very tight. This tight structure is excellent for gluing; loose fibers weaken a glue bond (like the weak link of a chain). The edges burnish up to a beautiful shiny finish because of the tight fiber structure. When wet it is the most pliant leather there is, and it holds a molded shape very well. In short, it is a superb leather in every way.

The first elkhide I ever saw was a white Alaskan elkhide jacket. It was hand laced with antler buttons and long fringe falling from the back and shoulders. When the fellow wearing it told me what it was made of I knew that elkhide was a material I wanted to work with. I was not disappointed when I finally got some. Elkhide has a fluffy, almost spongy fiber structure. It is very closely related to deerskin. Because it is a heavier leather, it is also proportionately stronger. The nap is coarser than that of deerskin, so it appears fuzzier from the flesh side. It has a wonderful feel. I have made braided elkhide ropes that I used to hang a leather swing. There has never been a more comfortable swing rope. I also used elkhide to make indestructible leather shorts for myself and the manager of an outdoor sports supply house. The first time my shorts got really dirty I washed them in a regular washing machine with warm water and then let them air dry. When they were dry they felt so stiff that I was not at all eager to put them on again, but when I did they softened up very quickly to better-than-new consistency. Elkhide is usually about 4 to 5 ounces thick, but as I mentioned before, I have had elk shoulders over an inch thick. So far nobody has come up with a good use for 1-inch-thick elkhide, but it's a good conversation piece. (I hear that hippopotamus skins are a righteous 2 inches thick.)

Talking about heavy leather, moose is pretty amazing. Moose are the largest native North American mammals. They have been known to derail freight trains by charging at them head on in defense of their territories. Naturally they have very thick skins. My elf shoes are made of 8-to-9-ounce moosehide. They are very soft and comfortable, and show no sign that they intend to wear out. Similar weights of elkhide and moose are practically indistinguishable from each other, except that the moosehide is a bit more dense.

Chamois originally was made from a particular species of goatlike mountain antelope (*Rupicapra rupicapra*) indigenous to the Alps. The soft, absorbent skins were highly valued as washrags. Well, the supply could not keep up with the demand, so chamois is now made from sheepskin (washrags being more important than genuineness). The sheepskin is not as strong, but there is enough to go around. Chamois leather is made by the oil tanning process so it is completely washable. It is widely used for making lightweight leather shirts, halter tops, and bikinis.

Sheepskin has a very delicate grain and fiber structure. It is the tissue paper of the leather world. Lightweight sheepskin (this includes sheepskin chamois) can be ripped pretty easily in your bare hands. It is generally unsuitable for garments because it is so weak. Even with this drawback it is widely used, because the flesh side can be made into the smoothest, most velvety suede. I recommend it only for areas of zero stress: hats, linings, appliqués and inserts. No sheepskin can withstand as simple a stress as that exerted on a pocket. The longer the wool was on the sheep the more fragile the skin is. Sheep with very long wool require practically no protection from the skin itself. Sheepskins are available with the wool left on, in which case they are known as shearlings. The wool is often more valuable than the skins so the skins are sheared before processing, thus the name. Shearlings are available in various wool lengths: from a quarter inch to one and a half inches most commonly and up to seven or eight inches on Icelandic sheepskins. Shearlings are probably just a little bit stronger than regular sheepskins, as the grain has not been exposed to any weakening chemicals. The difference is quite negligible; you really can't expect any sheepskin to be very rugged. Shearlings can be very useful because of their insulating and cushioning qualities. Coats made from shearlings can keep a person quite warm in the coldest winters (depending on the wool length, of course). To compensate for the weakness of the material, reinforcements must be made at every point of stress (pockets, shoulders, buttonholes and buttons), and as long a stitch as possible should be used so the skin won't be weakened by the perforation points. (I have been referring here to "woolly" sheepskins. A distinction must be made between these and the so-called hair sheepskins: capeskins from South Africa, cabrettas from South America, and some Middle Eastern sheepskins. These are notably stronger, although they are still weaker than goatskins or deerskins of comparable weight.)

Pigskin is characterized by its triplet grain pattern. It is commonly used for commercial gloves and bags. The skins are generally two to twelve feet and may be either chrome-, vegetable- or oil-tanned. Chrome- and oil-tanned pigskin can be very soft. Vegetable pig has a firmer texture than vegetable calf or cowhide of the same weight. I have used very thin pigskin and have found it to be quite strong. Most pigskin is made from South American carpinchos or peccaries. One of the most unusual leathers in my collection is some unsplit, 13-ounce, chrome-sumac-tanned pigskin with nipples around the edge of the skin. When I found it at a tannery in Gloversville, New

York, I had no idea what I would use it for. Since then I have made: a green gladiator's cap with a row of crimson nipples running over the crown and one nipple on each side; a flexible hanging for my bottle of Dust Bug (antistatic record cleaner) fluid for one-handed operation; a pad to keep my thread-snips from rattling; the lid fitting on a bone box; a pair of giant shoulder-length gloves; slipper soles; insoles for my sneakers; welts and heels for elf shoes; and my current project, a quadruple nipple string base bow case.

As you can see, I don't just wait until I need a particular type of leather and then buy it. I buy anything that I really like whenever I can afford it. Then when I want to make something special I have a variety of leathers to choose from. Designs are as often inspired by the particular qualities of a leather as is the choice of leather determined by the design. I have a collection now that includes the thinnest and the heaviest of leathers, the most supple and the most rigid. I have suedes with fine, short, velvet naps and some with long, soft, hairy naps. I have horsehide and rawhide for molding. I have snakeskins and I have furs from old coats. I also have designs sketched which are just waiting for one last piece of leather that I haven't found yet. When I want to make something I just look into my supplies to see if I have what I need — I usually do.

When you are buying side leather you may notice a "TR" or "X" stamped next to the footage mark. These are grading terms. "TR" stands for "table run." This term applies to the majority of skins in any specific tannage. "X" is a lower grade, allowing scars and holes. Grading marks are not always present on leather. The best way to find out if the skin is what you want is to check it yourself. Look carefully for any spots where the grain is broken or weak. Spot any range markings to see if you can fit your patterns around them or incorporate them into your design. Make sure the skins you get are big enough if you have a specific project. Make sure that there is no crud sticking to the leather. Sometimes fatliquors rise to the surface of the grain, forming a white "spew," indicating a high concentration of fatliquors. Leathers with a lot of fatliquors are the highest quality tannages. A surface covered with spew is a sign of quality not to be confused with ordinary crud caused by negligence (dropping skins on the floor or dropping globs of finish on the leather). A light buffing is all that is necessary to bring out the beauty of the grain of leather that is covered with spew.

A trip to buy supplies can take most of the day even if you don't have far to travel. Make sure you get enough of everything you need and make sure you are satisfied with what you get. There is really only one way to tell if you really like a piece of leather. Feel the stuff.

Tools

Y ou cannot do any leatherwork without tools, and they should always be of the highest quality. The idea that primitive implements were crudely made must be rejected. The degree of finesse and craftsmanship displayed in a flint skinning knife, or in a needle made from the shinbone of a deer by North American Indians, is practically unheard of these days. At the most basic level a knife can be your only tool, and still you can achieve remarkable results if it is sharp and you attend to the project with patience and dedication. A needle and thread (with a homemade sail palm) added to the knife allows you a greater degree of sophistication and smoothness as well as more flexibility of design. A rag and a beveler for smoothing the edges of heavier leathers and an awl for stabbing holes for stitching could make a proud craftsman's tool kit complete. Of course, all of his tools in this basic kit would be the finest available, and would always be kept in top condition.

Where do you get the tools you need to do leatherwork? First of all, you should be aware of what you need. Then, when you see it, you'll recognize it. The sources range from florist shops (for mist sprayers) to railroad yards (for track section anvils), and include paint stores, art supply shops, sewing shops, jewelers' and watchmakers' supply shops, cutlery shops, antique shops, shoe factory auctions, woodwork supply shops, and hobby shops.

The majority of leatherworking tools are supplied by the

Tandy Corporation and by individual shoe findings shops and leather dealers. From these three supply sources you should be able to find Neolite and other composition boards for cutting surfaces, shoe cement, linen and nylon thread, basic hand tools, and hardware (rivets, snaps, eyelets, Chicago screws, buckles and nails), as well as leather and leather finishes.

Chicago screw

Tandy carries a wide line of leatherworkers' hand tools, most of which are made by Craftool. Although the quality is not as high as that of tools manufactured by Osborne or the B. L. Marder Company, many of their standard tools are perfectly acceptable and are offered at a lower price than anywhere else. Many individual leather dealers also carry a fair selection of the important leatherworking tools. Most of the tools sold by the individual dealers are genuine quality tools, as these dealers are responsive to the professional leatherworker's needs for quality. Shoe findings shops often have some used tools, which might help you cut costs a bit as well as offering tools which would otherwise be unavailable. These tools mostly come from old shoe repair shops and may have seen a lot of action, but many of them are still hanging in as functional tools.

As is generally the case with modern technology, in the area of tools we have receded as much as we have progressed. Old tools are quite often better than new ones, but they are hard to find. A day spent visiting antique shops and out-and-out junk shops may yield some useful, esoteric tools. Then again, you might find nothing. It is a matter of patience; the tool you want may be hiding in the gutter or under a pile of junk in an old barn, and it will turn up just when you least expect it — if you keep your eyes open.

Don't ignore the possibility of getting your tools straight from a shoe factory. I have frequently seen shoe factories listed in the auction pages of the Sunday newspapers, and following up these listings has always been worthwhile. It is always gratifying to find a good tool, but even if you don't, it is still a lot of fun to take part in the treasure hunt.

Basic Tools

I already mentioned a basic tool kit; a few additions might be in order. Here, then, is my list of "essential tools." You cannot assume that they will stay sharp, so proper sharpening implements must be included.

Knife: #2, #3, or #4 shoe knife.
Beveler: #2 or #3.
Straight edge: As long as you can get, up to seven feet (depending, of course, on the capacity of your work table).
Punches: #2, #4, #7, and #9 are all useful basic sizes.
Hammer: Any kind will do; ball peen for sandals.
Awl: Even a big needle stuck in a handle will do.
Sail palm: Make your own, using a stone for the thimble to save money. Convert a commercial sail palm if you can afford it.
Needles: "Boye" 1/0 wool darners, harness needles, assortment pack.
Thread: Waxed nylon or linen. Nylon is best. Try to get a range of sizes.
Waterproof sandpaper or assorted stones.

This is a suggested list and is only intended as a loose guide. Build up your tool kit gradually; there's no big rush unless you plan to retreat from civilization (in which case you should be making all your own tools).

Odds and Ends

Oil cans: For sewing machines and honing oil.
Pushpins: You will never regret having a few extra pushpins.
Pens and markers: Bic ballpoints, Sheaffer or Wearever car-

tridge-type fountain pens, Flair and El Marko markers, tailor's chalk, tailor's soap markers, grease markers (white grease pencils are best for leather and suede). Don't buy nylon-tip pens, they are ruined by grease in the leather.

Notebook: It is a good idea to have a notebook in which to draw design ideas, phone numbers, addresses, and notes. Another system (which I have been using while writing this book) is to keep a number of index cards held together with a Bulldog clip. (Keep good notes on what you do and perhaps you will have material to write a better book than I have.)

Pattern board and paper: Posterboard, brown paper, newsprint, railroad board, Bainbridge board, shirt cardboards — all are useful for patterns. For more permanence, heavier material should be used. Masonite and Plexiglas patterns will last practically forever; Plexiglas has the advantage that imperfections in the material to be cut can be seen through it. Both Masonite and Plexiglas can be used as guides for direct cutting.

Knives

There are several different knives made for the leather and shoe trade. The square-point shoe knife is the best all-around leatherworking knife and is sold in five sizes. The shorter sizes (1–3) give firm control and are easiest to sharpen. The longer blades (4–5) are useful for skiving strap ends on straps wider than 1 inch. The extra length of the blade makes it more flexible. Because of this you can keep the end of the blade parallel to the skiving board without scraping your knuckles. I would recommend a short knife to start with.

There are two grips for the shoe knife. For cutting lightweight leather (and for scoring very heavy leather), the knife is held horizontally. The thumb rests on the ferrule and the fingers are wrapped comfortably around the handle. The backs of the fingers rest on the work to keep the knife steady and to achieve the lowest possible cutting angle. This position is most

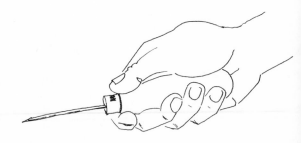

Grip for cutting lightweight leather

Grip for cutting heavy leather

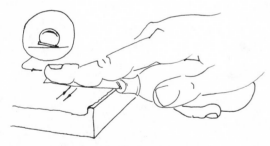

Sharpening knife on waterproof sandpaper with back-and-forth motion. Inset shows angle of blade

efficient because the cutting is spread out over the entire length of the blade. When cutting curves, efficiency must be sacrificed for maneuverability by lifting the handle so that only the point is doing the cutting (about a 45-degree angle).

For cutting heavy leathers (sandal soles, belt leathers, etc.) the knife is held vertically by placing the end of the handle in the V between the thumb and first finger and wrapping the fingers firmly around the handle. The heel of the hand should rest on the material. You will find that this is a very steady way to hold the knife when pulling the blade through heavy leather. For accuracy on extremely hard leather, it is best to score the cutting line lightly first, with the blade in the horizontal position, and then follow the scoring with the knife in the vertical position.

Your knife is your most important tool, so it is imperative that you learn how to sharpen it well. The idea is to get the blade so thin that it can slide right between the molecules of the hide without displacing them. A sharp knife is bliss, a pleasure to use; a dull knife is a leatherworker's bane. It will drive you crazy if you try to cut leather with a dull knife. To get my knife really sharp, I start with a medium-grit waterproof sandpaper (about 240–380 grit), which I dampen with my mist sprayer. I sharpen the blade using a straight back-and-forth motion. The angle of the blade to the sandpaper must be very low to create a narrow wedge. It should not be more than the wedge angle of the blade itself. The wedge of the blade on the shoe knife is about 7 degrees. This means that the top surface of the blade should be 14 degrees or less from the abrasive. Eight or 9 degrees is probably best. The narrower the angle of the wedge, the easier it will be to slice heavy leather with it. However, to make a narrower wedge, more metal will have to be taken off the blade. Thus it will require more time for sharpening. For thin leathers the angle of the wedge is not as critical, so you can save some time by using a higher angle for sharpening.

Oilstones provide an excellent sharpening surface. They are relatively expensive, but since they last practically forever the investment is worth it. Avoid coarse stones such as the carborundum pocket stone. Both Washita and hard Arkansas stones are excellent.

Another factor affecting the ease of cutting is the smoothness of the blade. Minute scratches left on the blade by the sandpaper create a lot of drag and should be polished off for cutting thick leather. I polish my knife with #600 finishing paper. When I am done, I can see my reflection on the blade. Finally, I use a strop to take the burr off the edge and complete the polish. The strop is a strip of horsehide 2½ by 24 inches with a 6-inch handle on one end and a swivel hook on the other. Sometimes, if the leather is very dry, lightly oiling the blade will make the knife cut much more easily. In these instances I also rub Hubbard's Shoe Grease into the leather at the cutting line. This keeps the blade oiled automatically. Some salamis are also wonderful for oiling knife blades. In the words of Andrew Beal, head woodchuck of the Woodchuck Sandal Works, "When she hums she hums."

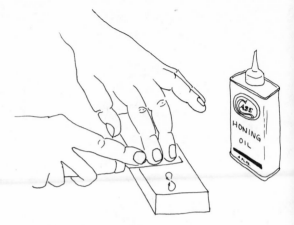

Use a figure-eight motion to sharpen a knife on an oilstone

X-Acto Knives

I use X-Acto knives to cut the slits for bound buttonholes and bleed knots, and to make slots on belts. Every once in a while an unexpected use also presents itself. The only blades that I have found really useful are #11 (fine point) and #17 (chisel point). This necessitates having both the large and the small handles. Scalpel blades are very sharp but too flexible to use on heavy leathers. When cutting slits, the cut should begin at one end and go to the middle of the slit, then repeat from the other direction. If the slit is cut in one stroke, end to end, the result will be one inaccurate end due to the angle of the blade. X-Acto blades can be sharpened. The amount of finishing paper required costs much less than a new blade.

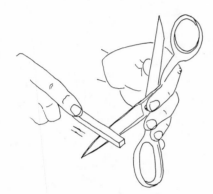

Dressmaker's shears and
toothed leather shears

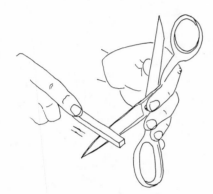

Sharpening shears with a
slipstone

Nose oil is the best lubricant
for shears. This is best method
of application

Scissors

Scissors are essential if you are planning to work with garment-weight leather. It is important to get the highest quality; bad shears just don't cut it. About the best and the most available shears are made by Wiss. I have a 9-inch Wiss bent handle, inlaid dressmaker's shear which I have used for years. Occasional resharpening is all it ever requires. Other shears I have used have been nothing but trouble.

Inlaid refers to a special edge forged from high carbon steel. Scissors made entirely of high carbon steel would be too brittle, so these specially tempered blades are inlaid on a more malleable frame. They are well worth the extra cost since they stay sharp so much longer than shears without this feature. The bent handles are also good to have. They allow you to cut on the table without bruising your knuckles.

If you buy Wiss shears, don't get the ones with the revolutionary new pivot screw. I have had two of these, both disappointments. Either I got two lemons or technology has failed again. Get the kind with the old-fashioned plain screw. Of all the shears that I have used, these are the best.

There are shears made especially for leather with a toothed lower blade, supposed to keep the leather from slipping. The leather doesn't slip, but it ends up with a lot of tooth marks. I stopped using them for this reason. They are mainly intended for heavier leathers anyhow, and I find that a shoe knife is better in any application where toothed shears would be used.

Several other good scissors manufacturers exist. The first that comes to mind is Marks and Osborne. I have learned that whatever scissors you decide to get, it is best to try them out on the kind of leather you want to cut before you buy them.

It is possible to sharpen shears by hand, using a slipstone. Open the blades all the way and pass the stone over the narrow blade edges, following the original angles precisely until all nicks and dull spots are gone. It is very hard to do this well, so if you can find a good grinder it may be worth trusting your shears to him for sharpening. Ask your barber who does his grinding.

Bevelers

Bevelers are used for finishing the edges of straps, soles, sculpture, and other pieces made of hard leather. They can also improve the appearance of lighter articles made of a compact leather such as a vegetable-tanned English kip. Bevelers are not suitable for mushy leathers. The beveler takes off sharp corners to prepare for finishing.

Bevelers come in several sizes. Either a #2 or #3 will serve as an all-around tool for limited budgets. For very thin leather

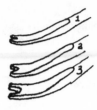

Different size bevels

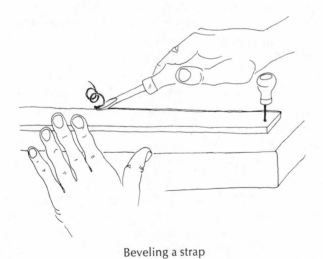

Beveling a strap

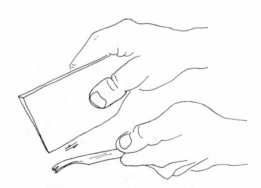

Sharpening a bevel with a tapered slipstone

(under 4 ounces) a #1 beveler may be required. Osborne and Craftool both make satisfactory bevelers. Bevelers can be sharpened easily with a tapered slip stone.

Skiver

The French skiver is essentially just an oversized edge beveler. It can be used to skive feather edges on leather up to ¼ inch thick. I use it in conjunction with my Formica block. Since the skiver will not cut into the Formica, it also can't gouge into the fine edge of the skived leather. This way I get very thin, even edges. This method works best with firm leathers that will not lift up from the block. The taper can be increased by making two or three additional cuts farther in.

The skiver can also be used to cut grooves for folding heavy leather. By bending the leather backwards over the edge of the block with the groove line directly over the edge, you can make an extra deep cut. Other uses are described in the directions that come with this tool of seemingly limitless uses. One function that isn't mentioned is removing strips of the grain side of the leather to prepare it for gluing, or inscribing messages ("made for Arlie Flotboggum by Ferd Snurdly").

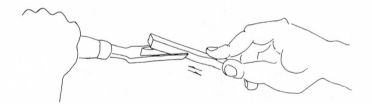

Sharpening French skiver with a ¼-inch-square slipstone

This remarkable tool comes with a sharpening tool which is also remarkable, if only for its ineffectiveness. I suggest a ¼-inch-square hard Arkansas slipstone. Well, okay, you can use the device supplied once or twice, until it wears out. It may not work so well by the second time. Another example of American ingenuity, folks.

The Osborne skiving knife is a wide, square-point blade with the square point sharpened. The skill required to use this straightforward tool is worth acquiring.

Skiving edges with French skiver

Gouges and Groovers

There are a few applications for gouges which the leather-worker may come across. Basically, they are used for decorative embellishment and as an aid in folding thick leather. There are gouges specially made for leatherworking, which are used with a pulling or drawing motion. They are called groovers, and consist of a shaft with a hole at the tip, one edge of which is sharpened. These give a very consistent cut, lifting off a thin strip of grain much like the strips cut by bevelers. Some groovers are made to cut strips at a specific distance from the edge of a piece of leather, and this distance is adjustable. These groovers are poorly made, in general; the adjusting screws wear out, or the shaft comes loose in the handle, or the tip which does the cutting breaks entirely, making the tool useless. There is also a groover made which is quite durable, though not adjustable. With a steady hand, nonadjustable groovers may be used in place of the adjustable type for cutting strips from next to the edge of a piece by using the thumb as a guide.

The French skiver is, in its way, a sort of gouge, although it makes a very shallow cut. This can be compensated for by bending the leather up to meet it, thereby achieving a deep channel. Ordinary U-shaped wood gouges and fishtail curve gouges are perhaps the best of all the gouges. They are the simplest and the easiest to keep sharp, although they require a good deal of control. Whereas the U-shaped gouge is mainly used to produce decorative effects, the fishtail gouge is most often used for carving heavy leather such as sole leather. There is a U-shaped gouge sold by Tandy with an adjustable collar to control the depth of cut, but again, this is a frivolous contrivance that only gets in the way. Although simple tools require more skill, in the end they are much more practical, usually less expensive, and of better quality.

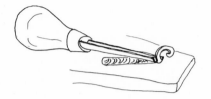

Gouge in use

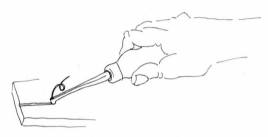

Groover in use

Rulers

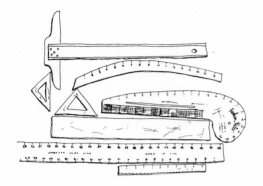

I have two straight rulers which I consider practically essential. One is a 12-inch flexible steel rule made by Lufkin. I have had it almost from the time I started working in leather. The other is a 48-inch steel rule made by Fairgate. These rulers have become so indispensable to me that when, on occasion, one or the other gets misplaced, I become disoriented and have a hard time working until it is found. Wooden rulers will work, of course, but the fact is that good steel rules just can't be beat for doing accurate work. Also, since they are so flexible, I enjoy flipping the ends up and down during a careless moment. The 12-inch rule doubles as my spatula.

The Fashion Ruler is another favorite of mine. I use it just about every time I make a pattern of any kind. This versatile ruler has a variable curve with ⅛-inch gradations on one side. It has a straight edge on the other side with a parallel slot and a 1 x 16 inch grid marked in tenths of an inch. It does everything. It also breaks easily. The Fairgate Vary-Form Curve Rule is more expensive but it has a more useful curve and will not break.

Then there is my heavy Plexiglas straightedge and hatband pattern. It is heavy enough (¼ inch thick) to hold down the leather securely for easy cutting, and the smooth edge resists the knife so well that the leather can be cut with the Plexiglas pattern held in place. The Plexiglas has the advantage, too, that you can see exactly what you're cutting. This is the best tool to use for cutting thin strips of soft leather from small skins.

I have several other straight and curved rules, but I don't get that much use from them and I don't feel that it's important to say anything about them. If you need a ruler that I haven't mentioned you will know better than I what kind you really need.

Hammers

I have close to a dozen hammers and as many different occasions to use them. I have listed and described briefly all the hammers that mean anything to me. I suggest you use whatever hammer is available until you find a better one for your purpose.

Ball peen hammer. The ball peen is the most versatile hammer for me. I use the ball end for hammering arches and texturing leather. The other end can be used for setting tacks and rivets, hammering nails, flattening seams, etc. It's a good early investment.

Wood or rawhide mallet. Punches, chisels and stamping tools should never be hit with a metal hammer because this flattens the shaft of the tool and eventually produces sharp edges where they're not supposed to be. There is no such problem with rawhide or wood mallets.

Rubber mallet. I use a rubber mallet to pound sandal soles together after gluing. Rubber mallets are lots of fun because they are bouncy.

French hammer. There are several French hammers made. They are characterized by their extended faces. This arrangement allows them to get into hard-to-reach areas. I keep one by my sewing machine for flattening seams close to the needle. When I make high-heeled sandals I use a French hammer to set tacks close to the heel. One French hammer distributed by the B. L. Marder Company has a unique arrangement of metal anchors to keep the head on and to strengthen the handle. (I don't have one of these, but only because of the price.) The handles on French hammers are subject to a lot of stress. The long head acts as a lever, which increases the force of the blow on the junction of the head to the handle.

Shoe hammer. Shoe hammers are made for cobblers. Some shoe hammers have a raised pattern on the striking face. This keeps it from slipping when it hits the tack. Others have smooth faces. The heads are usually set on at a peculiar angle that was developed to correspond to the height of the cobbler's anvil.

Some have straight heads. Different cobblers have different methods and equipment. All sandalmakers are familiar with this hammer.

Fiberglas handle shoe hammer. This is the only hammer with a really strong handle. It's great, but it's ugly. This problem can be remedied by any leatherworker with an aesthetic mind (that should include all of you) simply by covering the handle with leather.

Magnetic tack hammer. Far out, what a great idea! You can pick up the nails, start them, and drive them in all with the same tool! It doesn't work with brass nails. I stopped using steel nails two years ago.

Lignum vitae mallet. The name means wood of life. It is the densest and therefore the heaviest wood. It makes beautiful mallets that are best for pounding seams flat.

Heavy hammer, or maul. For driving those big arch punches through thick leather, you need something heavy.

Funny hammer. Well, we leatherworkers need a bit of comic relief now and then. I bought this hammer used from a shoe findings supplier. Hammers can usually be purchased second-hand and broken handles can always be replaced. Every hammer has a distinct personality. Try to find one that's compatible with yours.

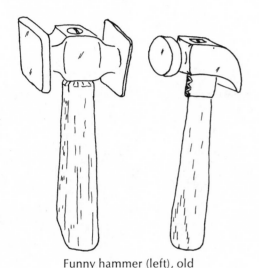

Funny hammer (left), old shoemaker's hammer (right)

Awls

I would not be without a good awl. Awls are easy to come by. They can even be made by inserting a big needle into a suitable handle. A small scratch awl is available now for about seventy-five cents. A better awl is one with a replaceable haft. Hafts come in many styles; the straight stabbing awl with a good polished surface is probably the best for all-around use. There are curved tips, diamond tips, triangular tips, and tips with eyes. Osborne makes good awls, and the B. L. Marder Company also lists excellent awls in their catalog. I have acquired several awls, some of which I use only rarely; these I have stuck in the wall and use to hang objects on (sort of like oversized push pins). I have patterns, tapemeasures and treasure pouches hung on them. I keep one awl at the right front corner of my cutting table. In this position I use it to secure straps which I am beveling. This leaves both hands free to guide the work. Heavy spring clamps also work without leaving holes in the strap ends, but they have a tendency to slip, and the awl in this position is immediately accessible for other operations (such as marking cutting lines). I have another hole at the left-hand side of the cutting table to use when I am cutting lace. Awls (and other sharp objects) are best left in their holes.

One of the uses of an awl is to pick out stitches that for one reason or another are undesirable. Also, it is used for pulling the ends of the threads to the back of the piece for tying off. For this purpose I have one awl which I keep in a hole on my sewing machine. This awl has a fine, blunt point so that it won't snag on the threads (like harness needles). Blunting is achieved by rotating the point while describing a circle on an abrasive surface. The tool is started nearly horizontal and brought slowly to a vertical position, each rotation raising the tool slightly.

When is an awl not an awl? When it is a fid, of course. Fids are used for tightening knots and straightening braids. They are also used for enlarging holes for lacing. It is actually just a specialized awl with a flat, tapered haft and a blunt point. I like the Osborne fid because it is very smooth. Almost any awl can turn into a fid in an emergency.

I almost forgot the awl for all. This awl started me out on the road of hand stitching. It is an awl with an eye at the end and a bobbin of thread stashed in the handle. With it one can make a perfect lockstitch with a little practice. There is also a stitching awl made under the name Speedy Stitcher which doesn't work as well as the awl for all, or the Osborne stitching awl. (Speedy Stitcher waxed nylon thread, on the other hand, is great.)

Sail Palm

Using a sail palm

The sail palm got its name from the sailmakers, who used it to help them push heavy needles through the unyielding canvas of the sails. Perhaps no other tool becomes as much a part of the craftsperson as this. Subjected to all the movements of the hand, this tool responds by becoming closer and closer in form to the hand that wears it, becoming an extension of the hand itself. With it you can sew the heaviest materials with ease. On these materials, it is true, holes must be prepunched with an awl. On lighter leathers prepunching is unnecessary. To accompany the sail palm you should have pliers for pulling the needle out of the material. I use a pair of lineman's pliers that I found on the street. The jaws have parallel grooves into which the needle fits perfectly. There is a special plier designed for just this operation. It has parallel-action jaws with a groove running from back to front for the needle. Whatever you use, always hold the needle *in* the groove, not against the groove. This will keep your needle smooth. If the needle gets marred it won't go through the leather as easily. A strip of deerskin or other soft leather can also be used to pull needles. This doesn't give any extra leverage, but it improves the grip enough to be a significant aid.

The sail palms available commercially are terrible. I think they were designed to be used by chimpanzees or orangutans. Besides that, the leather on commercial sail palms is like cardboard. The only solution is to remove the rawhide and thimble section and set it on a palm made out of good leather. (I recommend horsehide) which is designed to fit the human hand. I have included a pattern for this (see page 156). Soak the rawhide for about fifteen minutes to make it pliable before sewing it onto the palm. It is most easily sewn on by machine. If no machine is available, take it to a cobbler or borrow someone else's sail palm and sew it by hand. Be sure to bevel the edges well, especially around the thumbhole, and oil the palm thoroughly.

I have also included my pattern for a padded palm (see page 157). This is used for pushing sharp drive punches and chisels through leather without using a mallet. In principle, it is the same as the sail palm. It is a bit wider, to cover more of the hand, and it doesn't use a metal thimble as the sail palm does. The small pad should be sewn to the front of the palm first, and the larger pad then sewn to the back. This way you don't have to sew through more than two layers at one time.

Punches

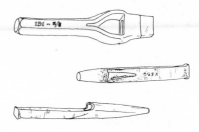

There are two distinct groups of punches, drive punches and rotary punches. Drive punches can be divided into several categories: round, oval, oblong, or special shape cuts; taper or straight-bore; cylindrical, offset, or arch-type head. A tapered bore is, of course, desirable so that punched blanks won't clog the punch. The cylindrical and offset heads are limited in size and are only made for round, oval and oblong cuts. Arch punches are made for any special shape or size cuts.

Top to bottom: oblong arch or bag punch; round offset punch; oblong offset punch

Rotary punches can also be broken down into a number of categories: ordinary pivot or parallel jaw; permanent or replaceable tubes and blocks; shaped-steel or solid-cast frames.

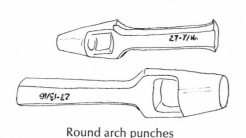

Round arch punches

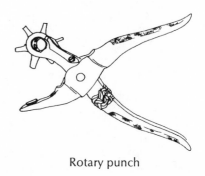

Rotary punch

When punching with an ordinary pivoting jaw, the tube meets the leather at an angle. If the tube isn't held firmly by the spring clip, it may click out of position and fail to punch properly.

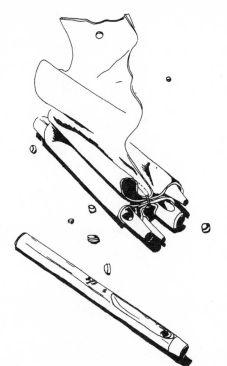

Drive punches held in sewn compartments in strip of leather

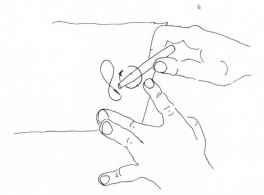

Sharpening a cylindrical drive punch with a figure-eight motion while rotating the punch

Parallel jaws do not have this problem since the line of force is straight up and down. Replaceable tubes are an obvious advantage if you have dropped your punch and broken one or two of the tubes. This advantage, however, is worthless when extra tubes are unavailable. (This has happened to me.) Make sure your supplier is dependable if you decide to spend extra for a punch with replaceable tubes. The cheapest rotary punch from Tandy works as well as any punch with ordinary pivot jaws that I've ever used — until the tubes break. The basic difference between the frame styles is one of cost. But I should point out that the solid-cast frame punches that I've had have been awkwardly designed and as a result very tiring on my hands. The handles are too close to provide the leverage necessary to do the job easily. If you're going to spend three to five times as much for an expensive punch, I suggest Sargent's parallel-jaw model with replaceable tubes. But if you're like me you'll forget about spending all that money on unnecessary tools.

I have Tandy's cheap rotary punch. Two of the tubes are broken. I keep five basic cylindrical drive punches (ranging from ⅛ to ¹¹⁄₃₂ inch) hanging in a strip of leather with compartments sewn in for each. I keep these punches honed so that I can push them through any strap leather with ease. I made myself a special padded palm which protects my hand when I use them. I also have an oval offset punch that I picked up for a quarter in a junk shop. I cleaned off the rust and I can make neat little oval holes on my belts with it. I have three oblong punches: ⅜, ⅛, and ⅝ inch. I have two round arch punches, ⁷⁄₁₆ and ¹¹⁄₁₆ inch, made by Krauter Tools. These I seldom use, but I enjoy having them when I want them. I specify Krauter rather than Osborne because the Krauter head has a smaller taper that makes these punches cut more easily. I have a set of four large arch punches, 1⅝ to 2 inches, that I rarely use, and finally I have a small strap end punch which I use for notching the edges of cowboy hats.

Punches can be sharpened easily. I use abrasive paper or an oilstone for the outside, and a pencil stone or a needle file for the inside of the punch. The punch is laid on the abrasive surface and moved in a circular motion while being rotated evenly between the fingers. I use a medium India pencil stone for most of my punches. But if the punch is too small for a pencil stone I use a needle file. Just a few strokes are usually enough to eliminate the burrs. A final polish may be put on the punch by wrapping a bit of finishing paper around the tip and twisting the punch back and forth.

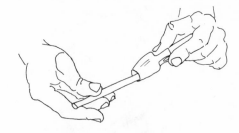

Sharpening the inside of the bore with a pencil stone

Needles

Needles are about as basic as you can get in the way of tools. There are many different kinds of needles made, almost all of which are useful at one time or another. The needles that I use the most are harness needles and wool darners. I get the largest size of each available, 000 (or three aught) for the harness needles and 1/0 (one aught) for the wool darners. The difference between these two is that the harness needle has a blunt point and the wool darner a sharp point. The harness needle also has what is called an "egg eye." It may be slightly stronger than the conventional needle eye, but I feel that the difference is negligible. Harness needles are designed to carry thread through holes which have already been made with an awl or a thonging chisel. The blunt point prevents the needle from snagging on the edges of the holes. Wool darners, on the other hand, will both pierce the material and convey the thread. They are used for sewing soft leathers in conjunction with a sail palm. Glovers' needles are specially designed to be used on soft leathers. They have a triangular shaft, the edges of which have been sharpened so that they actually *cut* a hole in the material. They pass through soft leathers easily enough without using a sail palm, but I don't believe in them. All the little slits weaken the leather considerably, and if you should repeat a stitch in the same hole the needle will sever the thread. This is not to say that they are entirely useless. Just make sure that you don't repeat stitches and use leather with good strength, such as deerskin, that won't be seriously weakened by the effect of the needle.

Now it is time to mention big needles. Sailmakers' needles, carpet needles, upholsterers' needles — all of these fit into this classification. Big needles come in handy in many instances, so they should not be overlooked.

I should also mention the "life-eye needle." This is a short pointed section of brass rod with the blunt end drilled and tapped with threads so that it can be screwed onto the end of leather lace. It is the perfect tool for threading latigo lace (like the stuff they sell for mountain boots at the outrageous price of 79 cents a pair, and which is really only 15 cents worth of leather). Life-eye needles can also be used to apply gold leaf to leather. Screw one onto a bamboo Japanese-style chopstick or other suitable handle, then heat it over an alcohol flame for a few seconds. Touch the heated tip to the backing of the gold foil placed face down on the leather. Reheat as needed. Curved life-eye needles are also available.

Sewing machine needles are made in so many point shapes that it is impossible to mention all of them here. Basically, though, there are two categories: cloth point and specialty point. The cloth point needles have simple round shafts and sharp tips. Specialty points are similar to glovers' needles in that the edges are sharpened. The same limitations apply.

The many different needle styles are created by varying the twist of the point, the number of sharpened faces, and the angle of the point. These differences affect the appearance of the finished stitch and the ease with which the needle passes through the material. My own choice is the narrow wedge point when I need a specialty needle. In most cases a cloth point suffices.

The finest sewing machine needles undergo approximately twenty separate polishing operations to reduce resistance and to prevent the overheating caused by friction. The benefits of polishing can be experienced on a small scale with hand sewing needles; the more highly polished the needle is, the easier it is to pass it through the leather. I believe in using quality tools and I feel that I cannot stress too much the importance of having good needles. The best hand sewing needles I have used are those made by the Boye Needle Company. The best sewing machine needles I have used are made by Beissel.

Strip Gauge

The strip gauge is a simple device for cutting straps of varying widths from a hide with a straight front edge. There are three types of strip gauges. The Dixon Company makes the plough gauge, the most sophisticated and most expensive ($40). The Osborne Company makes a hollow-handled, pistol-grip cast draw gauge, adjustable from ¼ inch to 4 inches with a quality steel blade ($15). The cheapest is a wooden draw gauge called the Strip-t-ease. It adjusts from 0 to 2½ inches and uses replaceable injector razor blades. Tandy distributes the Strip-t-ease for $1.50. I use the Strip-t-ease because it is cheap and works perfectly well on most all leathers with the exception of chrome-tanned belt leathers and horsehide over 8 ounces. The chrome leather dulls the razor blades very quickly. I had to use a dozen blades to cut the same number of straps. The horsehide was even worse; the razor blades just bent and broke. In both of these cases I believe the Osborne draw gauge with its sturdy steel blade would have been able to handle the job. This same blade, when fitted into the short knife handle, makes one of the finest leatherworking knives available. But since I couldn't afford it, I just replaced the blades while cutting the chrome leather and cut the horsehide with my knife, using a metal straightedge as a guide. This technique is used to make a straight edge on the side of the hide where you wish to begin cutting. If this is not done the strap will come out uneven. On mushy leathers the first inch of the strap will have to be cut by hand. To keep the leather from riding up on the blade (another cause.of uneven straps), hold it down with the thumb directly behind the blade. Since this makes the tool

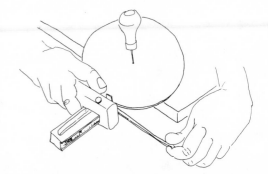

Cutting a long strip from a circle of leather with a strip gauge

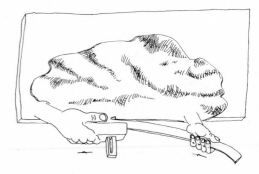

Hand position for cutting straps with a strip gauge

somewhat dangerous for your thumbs, I advise a firm grip. Cutting your thumb can be a disaster and will certainly hurt for a while. Pulling the end of the strap while cutting will keep the leather firmly against the handle and will insure a straight strap.

"The strip gauge is a tool used by beginners to cut their thumbs off." — Russ (Lefty) Gerard

Multipronged Chisels

Thonging chisels are used to prepunch slots for lacing and for stitching heavy leather with waxed linen or nylon thread. I never got into any decorative lacing, but I have used thonging chisels for stitching belts, bags and medium-weight garments. For lightweight materials I use a glovers' chisel. The glovers' chisel is simply a smaller version of the thonging chisel. As the name implies, it is used primarily for hand-stitched gloves. I would not use a multi-pronged chisel for any weak leather like cowhide splits or sheepskin. The chisel slots weaken the leather by 50 percent or more.

The chisel should be driven in from the front side of the material, or the side which is most conspicuous. It is very hard to get the chisel slots to come out absolutely even on the reverse side. When prepunching long seams, the first prong of the chisel can be inserted in the last previously punched slot. This insures an even stitch on the front. You have to be careful to keep the chisel absolutely perpendicular if you want the back side to come out even as well. If they are sharpened well, chisels can be pushed by hand with a padded palm, as with drive punches.

On very heavy leather, or if the chisel is dull, a mallet must be used. For flexibility on curves, it is desirable to have a selection of three thonging chisels: one-prong, three-prong, and, for long seams, a six- or eight-prong chisel. I have never seen glovers' chisels in any but one size; a stabbing awl may be used around curves on delicate leather. Multipronged chis-

Thonging chisels

els should be sharpened on a flat surface, taking great care that no prong is ground longer or shorter than the others.

Glue

Two kinds of glue are prepared for the shoe trade that can be used for most kinds of leatherwork. The first is nothing more than ordinary rubber cement. It is used for purely temporary bonds, where the leather is to be joined securely by stitching. This type of cement will not gum up the needle and thread as much as a stronger formula. It is also used for gluing seam allowances open. Since it loses its holding power quickly, it is not as apt to cause conspicuous ridges on the reverse side of the seam allowance the way a stronger glue would. Also, it is easier to use and dries faster.

Professional shoe cement is used wherever a permanent bond is required — any area where there is no additional reinforcement. It is used where great strength is needed and for bonding belt leather, shoe and sandal leather. On smooth leathers the grain must be roughened thoroughly if you want the joint to last. Shoe cement will provide a fantastic bond on suede without any special preparation. Sandpaper works well for roughing up light leather; shoe leather should be roughened with a rasp.

The first time you buy shoe cement get a quart can. The four-ounce can is too small to have any lasting usefulness and is much too expensive for the quantity you're getting. The brush in the quart can is a reasonable size, and the quart capacity is, too. The brush is good for precision gluing. The only trouble with the quart cans is that they are designed so that the brush never touches the bottom of the can. You can tip the can or fill it again before it's completely empty. By refilling from gallons, you can use the same can perpetually. There are also one-pint glue jars with adjustable brushes. These are available from

Tandy or most shoe findings shops. These brushes are over an inch wide (as compared with the brush that comes with the quart can, which is ½ inch wide) so they are not suitable for gluing small items like wallets. When I was making wallets on a wholesale basis I used a baby food jar to hold the glue. The brush from the quart can fit beautifully.

If you break one of the large glue jars it can be pretty messy, but don't throw out the cap and brush. The cap fits pint jars of Fiebing's Antique Dye, pint mayonnaise jars, and others. If you don't have any empty jars around the right size for the cap, just punch a hole in the cap of any jar and transfer the brush apparatus. Dark jars are the best since they protect the glue from damaging light rays. I have kept my original brushes in use through mayonnaise, baby food, acerola, lanolin, apple-sauce, and Fiebing's dye jars. Plastic glue jars are available which fit the standard cap and brush (good news for initiates).

After filling a smaller container from a gallon can, leave the cap of the gallon can upside down over the opening and wait until any drippings are dry enough to remove. Then lightly oil the threads. This will make the gallon can easy to open the next time. In the event that the cap gets stuck, a 10-inch pipe wrench will get the cap off easily. Shoe cement can be removed from smooth leather and work surfaces simply by rolling it off once it has dried. It is practically impossible to remove glue from suede.

Glue sticks (essentially just a sheet of dry glue rolled around a dowel) are made for picking up patches of dry glue. They will sometimes even take glue off very nappy surfaces by pulling the nap along with it.

In certain circumstances I have used Franklin's Tite-Bond and Liquid Hide glue with good results. Their limitations are their lack of flexibility. As long as you don't ignore the limitations you'll probably have good results.

Sprayers

Sprayers are good tools to have. Many liquid solutions come packaged in spray bottles (Windex, hair spray, glycerine saddle soap). You can use sprayers to apply dyes, but make sure that you have good ventilation and don't inhale while you are spraying. Spraying a mist of water in the air helps to keep down dust if you have a problem in that area. A sprayer is the best thing for moistening waterproof sandpaper for sharpening knives. Sprayers are good for dampening small areas of leather for tooling and molding. In short, sprayers have many practical uses. There are several types of sprayers available; old Windex bottles and such are good and don't cost too much. Florists and hardware stores usually have heavy-duty sprayers for about $1.50. My favorite sprayer is the all-brass mist sprayer sold by florists and mail-order houses for about $3. If you get one of these you will find it necessary to attach a pad of leather to the fingerhole for comfort.

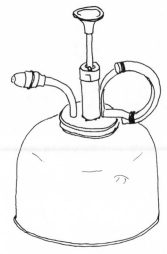

Brass mist sprayer

Lasts and Blocks

Shoe and boot lasts and hat blocks are forms over which these items are stretched and molded to give them the proper size and shape. They are usually made of wood or plastic resins. Both lasts and blocks are customarily used on special stands, upon which they can pivot around and around for easy manipulation. They are expensive when bought new, so it is best to seek them out where they lie from a previous use or user. Shoe factories dispose of great quantities of lasts when styles change.

Lasting Pincers

Lasting pincers are used to grasp material to stretch it over a last or other form. If you want to make conventional shoes or boots, you will need a pair of pincers. They, like boot lasts and hat blocks, are best picked up secondhand from shoe findings shops and shoe factory auctions. There are different styles made which include such features as tack hammer faces for tacking the leather without changing tools and tack pullers at the end of the handle. Some are made with the lower handle curved outward to give added leverage. They are worth having merely for their esoteric value.

Wrenches and Pliers

You may find it useful to have an assortment of wrenches and pliers about. Some have specific uses, while others just seem unpredictable in their use. A pair of grooved pliers will pull needles through leather after they are started with a sail palm. Needlenose pliers are good for pulling lace through holes and removing old stitches when doing repair work. A Stilson wrench (10-inch) is definitely the best tool for removing the caps from glue cans and for tightening all the nuts and bolts which are always coming loose.

By the by, most of my wrenches and pliers have come from junk shops or been found on the street or have been given to me by someone who had little use for them. (I can't imagine not having a use for them, but apparently it happens.) I leave you to your own devices to procure your wrenches and pliers.

Tack Pullers and Wire Cutters

As we are all human, we are all fallible. As tacks are only products of human industry, they also are not all perfect. Thus, in the course of hammering seventy-five to a hundred tacks into a pair of sandals, some will inevitably go in crooked. We are prepared. Two tools exist that can remove tacks. The first is the tack puller, a blade with V-shaped notches along one side and a notch in front. If the tack has not been hammered in the whole way, this tool is quite effective. When the tack has been driven all the way in, the tack puller cannot get it out without gouging the leather.

The other tool is an ordinary wire cutter. The best wire cutter to use is one with a flat lower face, the upper faces of the blade being ground to a bevel. This allows you to get closer to the leather. Wire cutters are the one tool that can remove rivets. They cut them in half, leaving two parts with one head each. And it is no problem to remove rivets when they are cut in half.

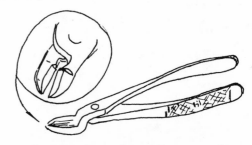

Wire cutters for pulling tacks

Staplers

For basting seams on bags and garments, beginners will find this tool especially helpful. I have long since outgrown my need for basting. Accuracy, experience and a developed eye eventually make it unnecessary. Staplers are most important in fitting garments, as will be described later. Almost any stapler will do, although for heavy leather an exceptional instrument made by Neva Clog is well worth looking for. This superstapler can even be used for permanent fastening if desired, although staples are not particularly attractive.

Snap and Eyelet Setters

Dot and babydot snap setters are spreading tools; they curl the ends of tubular posts or separate prongs. Eyelet setters are the same. These setting tools are simply inserted in the part to be spread and struck with a mallet. A concave anvil is used behind round-headed snaps to protect the shape. Bird cage snaps are assembled with a three-part tool: a two-way anvil designed to hold the bird cage or insert in the hollow stud back, a concave-headed tool for striking the cap of the snap to fix it to the bird cage, and a hollow-headed tool which fits over the post and is struck to fix the post to the stud back. If snap setters are struck too hard, the snap bends out of shape and becomes useless. I avoid snaps.

Stamping Tools

Stamping tools are used to make impressions in vegetable-tanned leather and latigo. (Other types of leather are too resilient to hold any patterns stamped on them. Moisten vegetable-tanned leather with a sponge, sheepwool dauber, or a sprayer before tooling to make it more impressionable. The stamps are struck with rawhide or wooden mallets to avoid flattening the ends of the tools. Formerly, a great deal of sophistication was developed around the art of tooling leather. Intricate patterns and floral motifs were prevalent in western cowboy leather tooling. Since then, looser patterns have evolved, leaving the leatherworker more freedom of design. There is less heavy stylization and more use of open areas. The accent is on design and form.

If you are interested in doing some tooling, the best idea is to look through a Tandy catalog of tools, and start out with whatever tools interest you. I am sure you will have no trouble developing your own style. Also, look carefully at tooling that other leatherworkers have done. It is always a good idea to expose yourself to as much of other people's work as possible, comparing things that you like and don't like.

Letter and Numeral Character Stamps

It's hard for me to say a lot to recommend letter and numeral stamps, but at some time you may have a use for them. If you get into wholesaling belts, for instance, you will probably want to have a set of numerals to stamp sizes on the backs of the belts. I myself use character stamps very infrequently. They are pretty expensive, which alone may discourage you, but if you decide that you want to get a set, here is an interesting fact. There are two ways of making character stamps. The first way (which isn't used anymore) was to cut the characters by hand at the end of a short section of brass or steel rod. The cutting was done with drills and files by skilled craftspeople who formed their characters gracefully and with flair. The second method, the modern one, is to cast the entire stamp out of steel. This produces a raised character on a flat ground. The character is only about $\frac{1}{16}$ inch high, which means that if the stamp is struck too hard an annoying impression of the ground will also appear. The old method of drilling and filing produced a stamp that made a clear impression with no external marks, no matter how hard it was struck. So look around old hardware stores, junk shops and antique shops to find an old set.

Shoe Rasp

The four-in-hand shoe rasp can be found at any hardware store. It was originally created expressly for shoemakers and repairmen, but it quickly became popular in many other areas, thus its wide availability. If you look at the shoe rasp you will understand the name "four-in-hand." There is a convex and a flat side for each of the two tooth arrangements, and since there is no handle it must be held in the hand. It is used to rough up surfaces for gluing and works very well for that purpose. It can also be used to smooth the edges of sandals; it is terrible for that purpose, but it does work, and it is much cheaper than a sanding machine. It is sometimes possible to pick up a used shoe rasp for about 50 cents; new ones cost a dollar.

Another type of roughing tool is made of hundreds of little blades stuck in a piece of canvas which is held taut on a specially designed handle. This tool costs $4. I got along fine without it for five years. It positively *cannot* be used to smooth the edges of sandals in a tight situation.

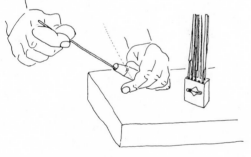

Using needle files to sharpen a drive punch

Needle Files

I don't know what I ever did without a set of needle files. I use them to sharpen tools, to smooth out rough spots on buckles and other hardware, and to shape metal, bone and wood accessories. The fact remains, however, that I got along without them for several years.

Seam Roller

I was first introduced to seam rollers by Stan and Susie Nichols when I visited them at the Sandal Shop in Hartford. They allowed me to do some work for them in return for their hospitality. I decided to make a few suede ties since they take so small an investment in materials (I was using their materials). I also knew that they could get a good price for them. Instead of a rubber mallet, they gave me a roller to press the glued parts. When I was back in my own shop I forgot about the seam roller until I decided to paint the walls. There was a display of many different roller models at a paint store, one of which caught my eye. It was a grooved, variegated, amber-colored wallpaper roller (Hyde model 313) with a slightly rounded face. I couldn't resist it. I have virtually stopped pounding seams or glued edges except in thick spots, and then only at the sewing machine with my lignum vitae mallet. My friend Mark got a roller to use at Happy Trails and this gave me an opportunity to compare different features. His is smaller, flat and has no grooves. The size seems to make little difference except in seam width capacity. I think the slight curve is good because it doesn't leave indentations at the edges. The grooved roller surface gives good traction, but glue tends to collect in the grooves, so sometimes I would prefer a smooth roller. Get a roller when you can.

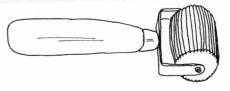

Hyde #313 roller

Brushes

There are several types of brushes which are used for leatherwork. The largest is the shoe brush. The best shoe brushes are made with pure horsehair. These brushes are good for buffing finishes to a gloss. Wax finishes really shine when they are brushed. I have found a shoe brush is the best tool for cleaning off my worktable. If you work with suede you will certainly want to have a good suede brush. The nap should be brushed up wherever it has been matted down by hammering or constant wear. The best thing for suede is a very stiff-bristled brush. The Dixon Company makes a number of acceptable models. My personal favorite is the Dixon #1215, which came from a shoe factory. I acquired it during an auction; it was a trifle which no one was concerned about. I also have a Dixon #232 which has soft steel bristles surrounded by stiff natural bristles as in the #1215. This has been useful for suedes of very fine nap. I got this brush secondhand from a shoe findings shop. It used to belong to "Hand the Hatter," who made the finest felt hats. I have a narrow brush, the width of about three stiff bristles, which I also use for suede when only a very light

brushing is required. I have a very stiff wire bristle brush with a long handle, another shoe factory auction acquisition. I use this brush after roughing up sandal soles to brush away the loosened fibers. I might as well say right now that I don't think too much of those brass bristle suede brushes they sell at shoe stores and dime stores. They tear the nap apart too easily. They are really only intended for rough shoe suedes, not garment suedes. A stiff natural bristle toothbrush is probably a good alternative to some of these suede brushes if they can't be found.

Large paint brushes (1¼-inch) can be used for applying oil (neat's-foot oil or melted mink oil) and also thick dyes (such as Fiebing's Antique Dye). Small paint brushes (³⁄₃₂-inch) can be used for touching up dye jobs with any kind of dye. They are very good for dyeing the edges of punched holes. Pipe cleaners are also admirable for this purpose. Glue brushes are really just paint brushes with special handles.

Brooms and Featherdusters

I especially love featherdusters. Featherdusters are very useful tools if you have a problem with dust. You don't know what dust is until you've worked at Laughing Alley. Well, maybe you do have an idea of how bad it can get. I have a plastic-handled featherduster which was extremely ugly, but I covered the plastic handle with leather and now it is beautiful. I even put on an elkhide strap to hang it by. Everybody knows how to use a broom.

Soap

Since I seem to be talking about cleaning up, let me recommend Lava soap. Lava soap gets dirty hands clean (you knew that already). I don't like to wear rubber gloves for staining leather. Minitman and some other brands of waterless hand cleaners actually remove leather dye from hands. Not only that, they contain lanolin, which is good for your hands.

First Aid

Don't bleed all over everything. Keep some Band-Aids around and some antibiotic ointment such as Bacitracin. Then cuts won't bother you so much when they occur (they *will* occur). I also like the new Micropore tape which can be used with or without gauze and some ointment. For really deep cuts (it can happen to you), invest in a box of large-size butterfly bandages. Many people have never heard of them, but they are the next best thing to stitches.

Finishing

Putting together a few pieces of leather and making something from them is really not very difficult. Achieving the dexterity to put them together smoothly and efficiently requires only practice. The true test of craftsmanship is the amount of time spent on finishing. Anyone can slap a belt together in a few minutes. A true craftsman spends more time on finishing than on construction. The craftsman spends most of his time making his work better: smoother edges, more supple texture, richer colors — all make a difference in the result. Working toward this end is always satisfying. Raw edges need not always be shunned. Raw edges (like raw vegetables) are often wonderful, but there is so much you can do with them. If you decide to leave raw edges in your work, make your decision for aesthetic reasons — because that is the best way of making a visual statement with the leather — not because you can't spend the time to finish them. Every facet of your work should lead to the perfection of the final product. Of course the satisfaction of making something perfect is very personal. Only the most sensitive people will appreciate the difference. The integrity with which you work is its own reward. Most people really can't tell how much work you've done on finishing because they don't know what is involved. What will be recognized are the quality of design and the basic integrity of your work.

As I've mentioned, there are three groups of finishes. The

different groups affect color, texture, and surface. I will deal with each group separately, starting with finishes which affect color.

Pigments are applied in the form of dyes. From my experience, the best dyes are made by the Fiebing Chemical Company. (I have had bad experiences with other brands, so I can't really recommend them.) Fiebing's makes two kinds of dyes: a thin fluid called "leather dye" and a thick gloppy kind called "antique leather dye," which for clarity I will simply call "antique dye." They also make a dye combined with a binding substance. This mixture is called "edge dye" and is used for darkening and burnishing edges of heavy leather. Dyes are always applied before other finishes. The other groups of finishes consist of lacquers, waxes, oils, greases, and soaps, all of which resist penetration by the dyes, to a certain extent, once they themselves have penetrated the fibers. Interestingly, oils and greases can also help to set dyes by acting as carriers. The oil or grease loosens excess dye and carries it deep into the fibers. Soaps have a similar effect, but they don't penetrate as deeply. They remove excess dye by washing it away.

The dyes are applied with daubers, sponges, rags, brushes, pipe cleaners, and so forth. Shearling daubers are best for all-around dyeing. Precut circles of shearling are packaged and sold for this purpose, but they are not worth the price of cutting and packaging. Scraps of shearling are sold by weight and are very inexpensive. If you are planning a project out of shearling — a vest, a jacket, or whatever — you can use your own scraps for daubers. In the process you will be eliminating some of your waste. A rectangle 3 x 4 inches is a good size to make daubers. To get them out of the way and off the dye table, punch holes in the daubers and hang them on nails. The dye table itself should be as smooth as possible to insure even dyeing. My own dye table is made of Masonite and has proved entirely satisfactory. Any small particles should be brushed off the dye table before dyeing, as they will leave impressions and dark spots on the leather.

The two dye types — leather and antique dye — are applied in different ways. Leather dye is a watery fluid, therefore it is best to place the dauber firmly over the mouth of the bottle, tip the bottle, and soak the dauber with dye. Antique dye, a heavy viscous fluid, is poured onto the dauber. It is not a good idea to pour leather dye onto a dauber. It is impossible to control the flow and it can become very messy. Once the dye is on the dauber, apply it to the leather with a quick circular motion for large surfaces or with a back-and-forth motion for linear areas, such as belts.

The solvent in leather dye evaporates quickly; as it does it lightens in color. The areas that lighten first should be gone over again before they dry until the whole surface appears uniform. Any surface residue should be removed with saddle soap when the dye has dried. Then the leather can be brushed up to a nice gloss. Another treatment involves allowing the dye to dry thoroughly, then brushing it vigorously and setting any remaining residue by oiling the leather well. The oil sinks deeply into the fibers and carries the dye with it. If you are planning to use a lacquer-type finish, oil should not be used because lacquer adheres best to a dry surface.

When using antique dye, the entire surface to be dyed should be covered very quickly to insure uniform initial penetration. (I become quite frantic when dyeing particularly large pieces.) Once the surface is completely covered, additional dye is rubbed in until the desired depth of tone is achieved. From here you can go one of two ways: either you can make the surface absolutely even in color, or you can create the antique effect unique to this dye. To achieve a totally even coloration, wipe off the moist excess dye immediately with a soft absorbent rag. For an antique effect, swirl or pat the wet dye over the base coat. When you have a satisfying pattern allow the dye to dry for a few minutes, then rub it down with a soft cloth. This is somewhat like finger painting. It is a lot of fun, and beautiful surfaces can be created. Watch the streaks as the pad moves.

Notice the completely different effect created by patting the dye on. Try sponges and other applicators for different effects. When the dye has completely dried it should be set with oils or coated with a neutral wax to protect the surface.

Antique dye is a more transparent finish than leather dye. The tones are lighter and seem brighter to me. The penetration isn't as deep, so the base coat must be rubbed in well to provide an adequate degree of permanence. For antique effects with very light colors, a base of leather dye may be used.

In nature, colors are blended in the evening sunset, in deepening shades of the forest, in a rainbow. In a leather shop, colors are blended in a bottle cap, a small dish, an empty jar, or directly on the leather. Blending colors is an entertaining challenge. It may be done to match leather to wood, to fabric, or to other leather. Colors may be blended to achieve richer, brighter tones, or to fudge it when you run out of a certain shade unexpectedly. All shades of brown are blends of red and green. More red makes a warmer tone, more green makes it deeper. (Fiebing's Mahogany Antique Dye is a rich reddish brown. Add some Fiebing's Green Antique to make a dye comparable to Fiebing's Cordovan Antique, except that it doesn't fade as quickly.)

Blending colors directly on the leather can only be done with antique dye. This method accentuates the first color applied. British tan with a coat of cordovan applied over it develops rich highlights. British tan is a very light color (a little more orange than regular tan), which would be overpowered by direct mixing with cordovan before application. Effective highlighting with light colors is one advantage of direct, on-the-leather blending. Another advantage is that you don't accumulate a lot of jars of special mixtures by mixing more than you need. Still another advantage is that you can try out each phase as you go, in the same way that you taste soup as you're making it.

When you mix regular leather dye, tests must be made on scraps that are allowed to dry before you can tell how it will work. This is time-consuming, but it may be the only way to achieve the color you want. Because the original color of the leather varies, the dye sometimes needs to be blended to compensate. For instance, navy blue on tan leather tends to be very dull. It can be brightened by adding a little bit of purple or a touch of red. Reds are improved by the addition of maroon or tiny amounts of purple. An eyedropper is ideal for this type of mixing.

Fiebing's Edge Dye is a highly penetrating dye that aids in matting down and sealing the raw edges of fibers to form smooth shiny edges. There are special wire-handled daubers made for applying edge dye. They are made with wool heads and felt heads. The felt heads give you more control. A small brush or a pipe cleaner works well for getting dye into small holes and other hard-to-reach places. Edges should be beveled before applying edge dye, if they are to be beveled at all. Apply dye to the edges after the surface has been dyed with leather or antique dye. This way, any edge dye that runs over onto the surface can be wiped off quickly without leaving conspicuous marks (remember, the dye acts as a slight resist). The edges are burnished by rubbing with a rag while the dye is still moist. Burnishing strap edges is best done by pulling the edge-dyed strap through a rag held in the opposite hand. Edge dye is available only in brown or black. The best substitute that I've found for burnishing edges in other colors is a mixture of mucilage and the appropriate color leather dye. Felt-tip markers can also be used to color raw edges in a pinch. I feel that a perfectly smooth edge is very desirable, so I often use two or three successive applications of edge dye to achieve the degree of finish I want.

Not all leathers respond well to edge burnishing. On latigo, for instance, the edges can be rubbed down until they're fairly smooth, but any wear will immediately make them rough and ragged. On very thin leathers, the high penetration by edge dye makes its use undesirable because it will spread in wide, uncontrolled stains around the edges. Antique dye penetrates very little and thus is much more suitable for thin leathers. Horsehide, on the other hand, absorbs edge dye evenly, burnishes quickly to a shiny smooth edge, and stays smooth for quite a while, even with constant wear. As you will learn, vegetable-tanned leathers are the most responsive to edge dye; the tighter the fiber structure, the more permanent the effect will be.

The second group of finishing substances are those which

affect texture. These are oils and other lubricants. They are often referred to as nutrients because they dissipate over a period of time and must be replenished to keep the leather mellow. (Oils also darken and impart a nice sheen to the surface of the leather, which places them in the third group of finishes as well.) Certain leathers need more attention than others. Vegetable-tanned leather, especially horsehide, can be ruined by neglect. Chrome- or oil-tanned leathers do not need the care that vegetable-tanned leathers require. At the same time, they lack a certain ripening quality found in vegetable tannages.

By this I mean that vegetable-tanned leather mellows with age and proper care until its personality and character have fully developed. If horsehide sandal straps were oiled every day that the sandals were worn, they would become more supple and more pleasurable to wear. Of course, every individual has different priorities, which may not include oiling sandal straps every time the sandals are worn. Oiling should be done when you are aware of the need, when you are aware that the leather is becoming dry. If a person's awareness is right then he will be rewarded by a lasting, beautiful work of leather. If his awareness is low, he will find vegetable-tanned leather possessions being repossessed by deterioration.

As a craftsman, your job is not finished when you have completed the construction of your design. It is your duty to make sure that products which you have created with patience and feeling will receive the proper care after they leave your hands. To do this you will have to try to judge whether the person in whose hands your creation will end up is sensitive to the needs of the leather. If the person is not, then you should not use leathers which would suffer from neglect for that particular person. If you decide that only horsehide is good enough for the recipient, you must impress him with the necessity of proper care. To this end, I often include a tube of Hubbard's Shoe Grease or a can of neat's-foot oil or Mermac mink oil with every finished piece. At one time I even mixed lanolin and saddle soap and included cans of it with horsehide strap sandals. However, I now feel that plain mink oil is far superior to such a mixture.

There are many different kinds of nutrient oils and greases and other lubricants available. Neat's-foot oil and Mermac mink oil are two of the most effective and convenient. Among the lubricants are coconut oil, codfish oil, olive oil, mineral oil, 30-weight engine oil (not highly recommended), and nose oil (not available in large enough quantities for serious oiling); greases including Vaseline, Hubbard's Shoe Grease, Sno-Seal, Dubl-Duk, and Dubbin; and unrelated lubricating substances such as silicone and glycerin. Neat's-foot and mink oil are both prepared especially for the treatment of leather. They are both commonly compounded with other ingredients such as silicone in order to make a less-expensive-grade oil. However, these compounds seem to impair the effectiveness of the oil; therefore, I recommend only 100 percent pure oils. Pure neat's-foot oil is a yellowish color and has a pleasant beef soup odor. It is made by boiling the hooves and shinbones of any of the bovine family — oxen, steer, cows ("neat" is the ancient term for this family). Basically, it is just clarified oil skimmed off beef soup. The best way to apply neat's-foot oil is with a brush 1 inch or 1¼ inches wide.

Mink oil is solid at room temperature, but melts when exposed to body heat. The only pure mink oil is Mermac mink oil. If you cannot find any, write to Mermac Manufacturing Inc., P.O. Box 5268, Salem, Oregon 97304. Mink oil is one of my favorites. Applying it with your fingers allows you to feel the reaction as it is absorbed by the leather. This is what makes oiling or greasing straps and laces such an intimate process between the craftsman and the leather.

Hubbard's Shoe Grease is another lubricant I have used a lot. It is darker and thicker than mink oil. It melts at a slightly higher temperature than mink oil, requiring the heat caused by the friction when rubbing it in. Hubbard's is sold in three-ounce cans and tubes. They call this "handy size"; indeed, the tubes make Hubbard's as handy as toothpaste. Hubbard's is similar to a lot of other leather greases. These are all sold as waterproofers for leather shoes and boots. Hubbard's claims "a guaranteed waterproofing. Sold on its merits." Each brand makes a similar claim and each seems to be a very good leather nutrient. Vaseline and other brands of petroleum jelly can be used in the same way. Silicone and glycerin also have some beneficial lubricating properties. Silicone is combined with oils and greases in commercial preparations. Fiebing's makes a liquid glycerin saddle soap which they package in convenient spray bottles.

So much for commercial preparations. Now for a little trivia. If you want to make your own supersauce, I have gathered a few recipes which may be helpful. Dubbin is a nutrient compound used by curriers (specialists in the art of leather dressing) for impregnating tanned hides to affect the texture and durability. Dubbin is traditionally compounded from cod or other fish oils and tallow or lard. One recipe (which doesn't call for tallow or lard) is as follows: A 10 to 20 percent potash solution is boiled and fish oil is added in a fine stream. Up to 50 percent of the mass may be fish oil. The mixture is stirred the entire time, and samples are tested occasionally until the mixture is totally homogeneous. The length of time varies; it may take several hours.

Beef tallow, mutton tallow, and lard were once important ingredients in curriers' leather dressings. They have not been entirely replaced, but one old-time ingredient has been banned from use by the federal government. Spermaceti is a waxy substance taken from the brain matter of whales. Since whales have been classified as an endangered species, whale products can no longer be found in the United States. One old formula called for 20 parts spermaceti, 40 parts wax, 30 parts pine resin, 50 parts turpentine, 400 parts linseed oil, 200 parts fish oil. Birch tar oil was used as an aromatic lubricant for leather in Russia in the time of Marco Polo. Times have changed.

One of the most important functions of the leathercrafter is the currying of vegetable-tanned leather, especially straps and laces. When you take on the role of the currier, you concern yourself (for the time) only with the perfection of your material, your ability to bring out its beauty. As I mentioned, this is the most intimate contact a craftsman can have with leather. After beveling the lace or strap, the edge fibers are set down with edge dye and burnished. Now the fun begins. Start with a large glob of grease or mink oil in your hand and work it well into the strip of leather. The heat of the friction built up by rubbing will cause the grease to melt and penetrate the fibers more easily. As the oil penetrates the fibers, the leather will become more and more pliable. Eventually you will be able to wind it around your fingers as you pull it through your hands. Keep the surface of the leather greasy. When the oil has penetrated completely you will be able to weave the leather in and out of your fingers as you pull. This over-under pattern breaks the "spine" of the lace or strap and makes it very flexible. The amount of time you spend oiling determines how flexible the leather will finally be.

The third group of finishes affects the surface of the leather. They protect the leather from moisture, clean off dirt, and give the surface a shine. This group is composed mainly of waxes, although lacquers are also used. Saddle soap is often used to clean the leather before applying waxes or lacquers. Many commercial wax preparations are sold as shoe polishes and come in various colors. The most popular ones are Meltonian and Propert's Shoe Cream. I have used Propert's quite a bit for putting a gloss on belts and on the edges and straps of sandals. Several neutral wax creams are available, including Leather Balm, Leather Balm with Atom Wax, Mello-wax, and the neutral shades of Propert's or Meltonian cream.

Propert's and Meltonian shoe cream are thick pastes. Propert's is packed in jars, Meltonian, in tubes. Leather Balm and Mello-wax are not quite as thick and they come in small-mouth bottles. Leather Balm with Atom Wax is thin fluid. It should be applied quickly so that it will cover completely with one application. Fiebing's also makes a wax preparation called "antique finish" (not to be confused with antique dye). This is a thick paste like the shoe creams. Unfortunately, it is sometimes used without discretion; when it is applied too thickly it has a tendency to rub off on anything and everything. After being applied, these paste or cream waxes must be allowed to

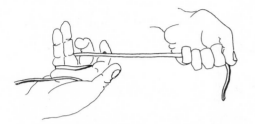

Breaking the spine of a lace

dry. Then the leather should be buffed with a horsehair brush or soft cloth.

Solid waxes are applied directly with the brush. The softer stick waxes are applied with hand or power brushes, while carnauba wax (the hardest of all waxes) can only be applied with high-speed motorized brushes. The waxes produce an unobtrusive light finish with considerable arm exercise if applied with hand brushes. First the wax is transferred to the brush by passing the brush over the wax with a vigorous back-and-forth motion. Then the leather is brushed until it shines. Carnauba wax is used mainly for burnishing the edges of soles. It is applied to the motorized brush and the heat of friction melts the wax coating the bristles. The sole leather then is moved across the brush to coat the fibers with wax, and then lightly buffed by hand or on the machine with a clean brush or wool pad.

Ordinary paraffin wax has a history of applications with leather. Roman soldiers wore armor made from leather soaked in melted paraffin and slapped on the soldiers' chests, legs, and so forth. This custom molding must have been extremely painful, but apparently resulted in very effective armor which had a high resistance to punctures. It is told that in medieval times soldiers on a crusade used lightweight leather boats that had been immersed in paraffin to catch fish during Lent. I once burned a candle in my shop that dripped wax all over a suede skullcap that I had on display. I couldn't hope to remove the wax from the suede, so rather than let a little wax ruin a skullcap, I decided to let it ruin two skullcaps. I stitched another skullcap to the inside of the first one as a liner and then immersed the whole thing in a pot of melted paraffin. I now use my waterproof leather bowl for breakfast cereal and thread snippings. If the skullcap had been my size it would have made a good helmet.

Beeswax can be applied like paraffin in a melted state. It produces a softer finish than paraffin. It should not be applied cold.

Construction Techniques

To describe the different methods of leather construction, I will divide all leather into three categories. First are those leathers that are heavy enough to be suitable for nailing with shoe tacks. This qualification is made only to categorize the leather; it makes no difference whether you decide to nail it, glue it, sew it, lace it, braid it or rivet it together. This category I will simply refer to as heavy leather. It includes anything of belt weight or over. Second are those leathers that are thin enough to sew easily by hand without making preparatory holes. These are called garment leathers. The third category encompasses those leathers that are too thin or just too soft for nails, but too heavy to sew easily by hand except by making stitching holes in advance. These are generally called bag leathers. Bag leather construction techniques are drawn from those of both heavy and garment leathers; no construction techniques belong uniquely to this group.

Heavy Leather

To learn the techniques necessary for working heavy leather, one might well start with belts and sandals. All the fundamental techniques are used in creating these items. The basic finish-

veler's bag made of 5-ounce oiled cow-
e. Balanced straps made of 8-ounce latigo,
ened with elkhide bleed knots. Internal
me made of steel rods for support

ing operations of beveling, dyeing, burnishing, oiling, and waxing are all performed in making a belt. Making sandals develops skillful cutting better than any other project, and also teaches the techniques of molding, gluing, and cobbling. Both belts and sandals require skiving and punching, and using the knife, French skiver, drive, and rotary punches. Practically all the methods of fastening leather to leather can be investigated: stitching, lacing, cobbling, riveting, Chicago screws, and even snaps. (This list is in order of my preference for the various methods; snaps are the lowest in my regard.) A simple three- or five-strand solid-braided belt can provide an easy introduction to the beautiful art of braiding and knotting. Belts make excellent surfaces for stamping and tooling. Most important, belts and sandals require only a small investment in materials and can easily be sold at a profit.

Belts

Let's begin with belts. First put a straightedge on the hide in order to cut a belt strap. Use a metal straightedge for marking (scribing) the edge of the hide. I use a 4-foot Fairgate steel rule, but any reasonably long straightedge will do (seven feet is best of all). The scribed edge is cut with a knife; straps can be cut with a strip gauge. To make the strip gauge cut perfectly straight straps, hold the material firmly to the crossbar, and pull on the strap as it is being cut. This steady tension pulls the leather up against the edge of the handle so that the width of the strap is constant and true to the measurements on the gauge. If a keeper ring is required, it should be cut at this time unless a large enough excess is expected on the strap.

When the belt strap is cut, it is beveled on both sides to round off the edges. When they are burnished they will feel smooth and will slide easily through belt loops. There is really no trick to smooth beveling besides a smooth, even handling of the beveler. To make it a bit easier, though, it is helpful to hold the end of the strap securely so that both hands are free to guide the beveler and to hold the leather flat as it moves along. The best way to secure the strap is to stick an awl through it and into the workbench at the right-hand corner of the bench. (Of course, a left-handed person would reverse this.) The only problem with this method is that it leaves a hole at both ends of the strap. In the event that such a mark would be undesirable I do not use an awl. Instead I bevel the first foot or so without securing the end of the strap. When the beveled part is long enough I sit on the strap as I complete the rest of it. I have never seen anyone else do this, but it is perfectly satisfactory. Spring clamps can also be used. They are a bit awkward for the first couple of inches, but are fine after that. Straps can be beveled without being secured. The hand opposite the one holding the tool creeps along holding the leather flat rather than moving continuously, smoothly forward. Don't be embarrassed; sit on it.

Any stamping or tooling that you plan must be done while the strap is in this raw state in order to achieve maximum effect. The leather is dampened thoroughly so that it becomes impressionable. Then it is either struck with tooling stamps or worked with simple modeling tools. The stamps should be struck with sharp, precise blows with a wooden or rawhide mallet. Stamping and tooling is overdone and done without feeling far too often. If you decide to experiment in this direction approach the problem conscientiously and with integrity. Try not to merely repeat what others have already done.

How the strap is dyed depends on you. Whether you use several applications of different, blending colors of antique dye, or one straight shade of leather dye; whether you make it streaky or even — it is up to you. Try to complement the buckle or any other hardware you use. If the belt has been tooled do you want to dye different areas of the tooling different colors? If the belt is for a particular person, try to fit the colors to the personality. Or take off on the mood that affects you and see what happens. Above all, have fun with the colors.

Now the strap is ready for the edge dye. To stand the strap

Lower three belts from left to right: too
hinge belt with decorative lacing ma
by my valued friend and teacher Ron Kro
horsehide belt with Russian foot soldi
buckle fastened with tapered strap end;
well-oiled horsehide belt with buckle
Dick Patters
Upper three belts left to right: Dinn
horsehide belt stamped to match buckle
Dick Patterson; Jason's belt made of hor.
hide and backed with kidskin, silver a
abalone buckle made in Mexico; Robert's b
made of 8-ounce shoulder, inlaid leatl
buckle made by Noah's Art in Montr

on its edge, curve it like a snake. The edge dye is then applied with a felt dauber. Watch the grain side of the leather as you're working to make sure that the dye doesn't run over onto the surface of the strap. As soon as each side is done, take a coarse rag in your hand and pull the strap through it, exerting pressure against the just-dyed edge. The sooner this is done the more effective it will be. A second application may be applied to both sides and then both sides burnished with a rag simultaneously.

At this point, the strap should be oiled or waxed. Remember that oiling subdues and darkens bright colors while wax highlights them. Oiling makes leather more supple and more resistant to the stresses of wearing. While most wax preparations contain some leather nutrients, they are not as effective as concentrated oils. My preference is oil on vegetable-tanned belt leathers and a light wax on latigo or other chrome-tanned belt leathers.

Once the strap is in its finished state the buckle may be attached (if one is to be used). Many buckles have loose tongues on crossbars for which slots must be cut. The slots must be wide enough to accommodate the base of the tongue and long enough to leave the tongue free when the strap is wrapped around the crossbar. I judge the length of the slot by eye with little difficulty. To make a slot, select a drive punch of the appropriate diameter and punch two holes where the ends of the slot will be. Then cut between the holes on both sides; these cuts should only be made halfway, then started from the other direction and met in the middle. This insures that the cuts will not extend beyond the holes.

If the belt requires a keeper loop, the center of the slot should be about 4 or 5 inches from the end of the strap. Otherwise it can be as little as 1½ inches from the end. I make keepers by wrapping the keeper strip around two thicknesses of the strap, then pulling the strap out of the loop thus formed and punching a small hole at the overlap. I skive the ends down on the flesh side, starting from the insides of the holes, progressing at an angle of about 10 degrees to a feather edge. This reduces bulk at the joint. A hard, smooth surface (such as

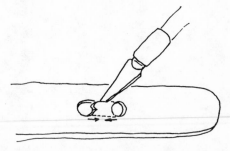

Cutting slots for belt buckle tongue

Fastenings for
keeper loop; rivet
and hand-stitched

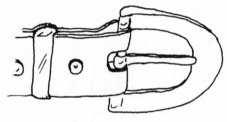

Belt holes

glass or Formica) is best for skiving work. I fasten the keeper loop with a small rivet (6 mm.). This is one spot where rivets prove their value. They may also be used satisfactorily to fasten the belt strap to the buckle. I generally prefer to hand-stitch in places that show in order to satisfy my aesthetic sense. For sewing belt-weight leather, stitching holes must be made in advance, either individually with an awl, or several holes at a time using a multipronged chisel. A blunt needle such as the Osborne harness needle is used to pass the thread through the stitching holes. The reason for using blunt needles is that sharp needles would snag on the edges of the holes. By making the holes individually, a free-form design can be made.

Two types of thread are suitable for stitching heavy leather. Linen thread waxed by hand is the age-old shoe and harness makers' thread. It comes in armspan-length pieces with fluffed, tapered ends. Boar bristles are traditionally used instead of needles, but only the oldest shoemakers still remember how to use them. Instead, harness needles are commonly used. The thread is first waxed by pulling it through a cake of beeswax, which lubricates the thread so that the fibers don't get snagged and holds the tapered ends together. When the thread is well waxed it is inserted in the eye of the needle. Then the needle is stuck through the thread above the eye and the end of the thread is pulled tight and rewaxed. Needles can be attached to both ends at once for saddle stitching. The tapered ends on the linen thread eliminate bulk at the needle eye so the thread will pass through the hole easily.

Nylon thread has superior strength and, even more important, will fuse upon application of heat. This makes it possible to end the stitching in such a way that it positively will not come apart. This is not so important for belts, in which stress upon the thread is minimal, but as far as I'm concerned it is practically essential in many other items.

To fuse the thread, I first tie it in a square knot (a square knot is the best though others will work) and snip off the ends. Then I heat the knot with a match until it begins to melt. As it melts I withdraw the match and press the molten area lightly with my fingers to flatten the knot. This leaves a tiny button of nylon with a fingerprint. To smooth out the fingerprint, I bring the match back over the little button of nylon just until the surface is smooth. When the thread is very bulky I often repeat the process of melting and pressing down the knot several times to achieve the flatness I desire. Care must be taken to avoid melting away the threads leading to the knot since that would eliminate any strength gained by fusing the knot. Also, a bit of experience is necessary to know exactly when to press the molten thread so that it will shape easily without burning your fingers (molten nylon can be very hot).

The technique for tying off linen thread is not very different. I bring the ends of the thread between the two layers of leather and then tie the knot so it will be as inconspicuous as possible. Then I smash the lump caused by the knot with a hammer so that it doesn't bulge. If you are attaching a keeper, the belt strap must be fastened on either side of the keeper to hold it on. Fasten the strap close to the buckle first, slide the keeper on, then fasten the strap on the other side of the loop. The holes for this second fastening should be made with the keeper in place for accuracy. When bending the strap around the crossbar on the buckle, it is a wise precaution to wet the leather at the line of the bend to help prevent cracking. If the strap is heavily oiled, of course, water will not penetrate. In this instance additional oil may be applied at the line of the bend if necessary.

The measurements on a belt are made from the point on the tongue where it passes through the hole to the hole through which it passes. I generally make one hole an inch farther than the desired length and two or three holes closer. This allows for the stretch of the leather and for any weight changes on the part of the wearer. When the holes are punched I hook the buckle to the farthest hole and mark the spot to be cut off as the end. Enough extra length should be left so that all the stitching, lace, rivets, etc., are covered. The end may be cut round, at an angle, or (as I usually do) with both corners cut at about a 30-degree angle. If you do this, the best way to have

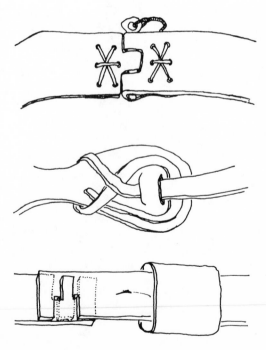

Belt fastening designs

it come out even is to cut one corner first, then lay the cut piece next to the other edge as a guide.

Many different styles of belts can be made which require no buckle at all. These are simple to make, inexpensive (it eliminates the cost of the buckle), and fun to devise. In addition, the aesthetic satisfaction of a belt made entirely of leather or leather with a wooden peg, etc., is immense. Only a few methods are shown here. Keep your eyes open and your mind free and you are bound to see or invent others.

Braided belts are beautiful and fun to make. The method of making a solid braid is probably the most familiar trade secret of leatherworkers. For some reason the technique is rarely demonstrated, although it is quite simple. I will discuss braiding in some detail at the end of this section.

Sandals

Making sandals will not only teach you many techniques of working with heavy leather, it is also a great way to get into production leatherwork. Every summer a lot of people buy sandals, and many of them like the idea of having a pair custom made for them. The sandal business has a definite season from about the end of March to September, with peak activity in June and July. Sandals are relatively easy to make and do not use a lot of material. In addition, the going price of custom sandals makes it quite profitable to get into making them. Even if you don't care to go into business, the comfort and satisfaction you will get from your own sandals will certainly be worth the time you spend on them.

What follows are the methods that I use for making sandals. My methods have always been open to change, and I intend them to serve only as good guidelines to get you started.

The first step is to see whether both feet are the same size and shape. If they are it will be necessary to trace only one foot and to cut only one pattern. (Simply reverse the pattern to cut the sandal for the opposite foot.) The predominant foot is usually larger and therefore should be used for the pattern.

Sandalmaking setup: anvils, arch block, nail tray, rasp, glue pot

However, if visible structural or size differences exist between the two feet you will have to cut two separate patterns. To begin, trace the foot accurately on a material such as poster board or shirt cardboard. The body weight should be evenly distributed on the foot. I usually have customers stand with their feet about shoulder width apart. This distributes the weight well and allows me to reach all around the foot to trace it easily. The outline of the foot is drawn with the pencil absolutely straight up and down. It is especially important to keep the pencil perpendicular at the heel and toe, otherwise the sandal is liable to be too short. After drawing the outline of the foot, the arch and strap locations must be marked. To place the arch accurately, I mark its center and measure its height. Then I drop the pencil from the perpendicular to trace the curve inside the arch.

For marking strap locations you have to decide what style you are going to make. This decision depends on personal taste, need for support, and whether socks are to be worn with the sandal (no toe straps in this case). I like to base the

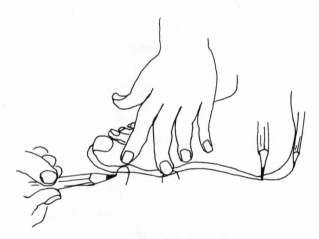

Trace foot, feeling out strap positions

decision on the foot itself, wrapping my fingers around the foot and feeling the various ways that the straps would naturally fit. Take off your shoe and look at your foot. You will notice on the inside of the foot there is an indentation just behind the wide part of the big toe and another indentation behind that. Place the thumb of the hand corresponding to the foot (left foot, left hand) in the second indentation and grasp the foot. Now move your hand backward toward your heel. You will feel a lump which is the joint of the first metatarsal bone. The outside of the foot is much the same as the inside except that the bones are much smaller. All of the indentations and protrusions are useful for holding a sandal on with properly placed straps. Improperly placed straps can pull a

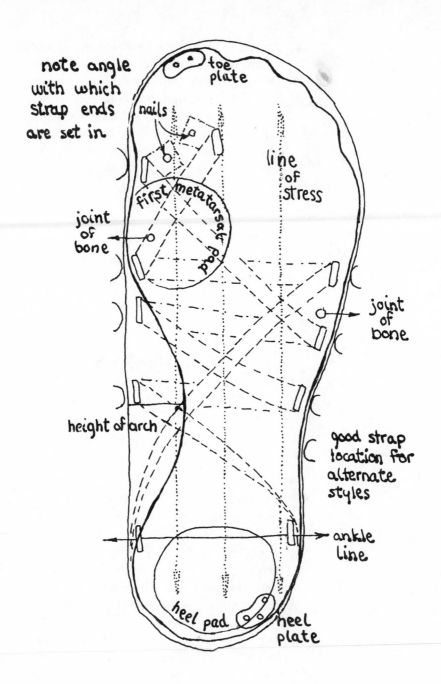

note angle with which strap ends are set in.

toe plate

nails

first metatarsal pad

line of stress

joint of bone

joint of bone

height of arch

good strap location for alternate styles

ankle line

heel pad

heel plate

sandal out of line with the foot. To avoid having a sandal twist on the foot, the straps must be balanced correctly. The sandal should fit naturally without twisting even when the straps are loose. This is the sign of a well-balanced strap arrangement. The angle at which each strap crosses the foot affects the balance. The straps tend to assume a position straight across the foot. Another way of describing this is that the foot tends toward a position perpendicular to the strap. An angled strap, then, shifts the position of the sandal unless it is firmly anchored in indentations at each side. To arrive at a balance, opposing straps are added. This is simple to demonstrate by drawing a strap pattern and bisecting each angle where two straps intersect. The bisecting lines will give you an idea of how well the foot will be held in line. Wide cross straps must be placed with judgment since they have a greater influence than narrow straps. The foot pattern here shows my way of marking strap locations with a U while tracing the foot, and then indenting about ¼ inch for the strap slot. Remember that the *outline* is made with the pencil perpendicular; *indenting* for the strap slots is necessary to account for the inward curve between the outside edge and the sole of the foot.

When the tracing is complete I add a border of about ¼ inch at both the heel and toe to allow for some sliding back and forth. This addition can be made by eye while cutting out the pattern. In the interest of a more graceful product I do not add any border to the sides. After cutting out the pattern, the strap slot locations are punched out with an oblong punch so that they can be marked on the topsole. Then the pattern is transferred to the leather. Remember that the bottom sole should be drawn on the flesh side of the leather or on the grain side, but with the pattern upside down. This leaves the flesh side, which is suitable for gluing, facing the flesh side of the topsole when the two layers are put together. Mark the strap slots on the topsoles, not on the bottom soles; you don't want to punch holes on the wrong side. For cutting efficiency you can place sandal patterns close enough to each other to eliminate practically all excess. Cutting lines can often be common to two soles. An entire soling bend can be reduced to just a handful of small triangular pieces in this way.

Cutting out soles is especially difficult around the tight curves of the toe and heel. I used to have to make a lot of extra cuts around the curves and use several strokes to cut through the leather. I can now cut sandal soles with one cut exactly along the cutting line by raising the angle of the knife at the curves so that only the point is cutting. An old knife whose blade has been worn narrow also turns more easily at curves. Since the knife tends to follow the random direction of the fiber structure in the leather, a shallow starting cut is sometimes necessary to keep the blade from drifting from the cutting line on very tough leather. If the leather is very dry, the knife won't cut as easily; it will squeak and grab the blade. To overcome this problem I make a shallow starting cut and then rub grease on the cutting line. With the heel of the hand braced on the leather the blade of the knife can be pulled along by the fingers with great precision. Cutting soles by hand gives you calluses on your fingers. I used to cut soles with a bandsaw, and before that with a jigsaw, but experience has shown me that a knife and a strong hand are the most efficient cutting tools.

After I have cut out the soles I throw them in a bucket of water. After thirty minutes to an hour I remove them from the water and let them set for about twenty minutes. This drying period is known as "samming." For some reason the leather becomes more responsive when the moisture has partially evaporated. If I am working on a lot of soles at once I stack them. This way evaporation occurs only at the top of the stack and the moisture is retained. This period of soaking and samming is a good time to prepare the straps.

When the soles have sammed to a good working consistency, I punch strap slots and mold the arch. I like to punch oblong slots for the straps with about the same dimensions as a cross section of the strap. I believe that this lessens the possibility of stress on the slot. I have a number of friends who prefer to make a chisel cut slightly wider than the strap. They say that the problems I imagine with this method do not exist.

So it is really a matter of personal preference. However the slots are cut, with chisels or oblong punches, they should be made at an angle to follow the curve of the foot. This eliminates sharp bends of the strap, which would have a weakening

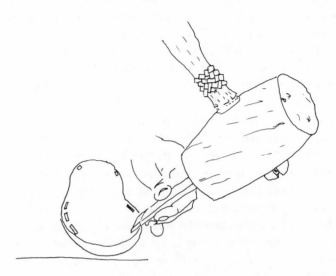

Cutting strap slots

effect. I carry this one step further and skive the inside edge of the slot on the flesh side with a French skiver. Now the arch may be molded.

Skiving inside edge of strap slot

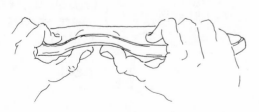

Molding the arch

Molded arches are not merely bent into the proper shape, they must be stretched. Remember that the pattern is made of the entire foot on a flat surface. The arch is merely indicated on the pattern. If the area of the arch is merely bent upward, the outside edge of the sole will take on a curved shape incongruous with the actual shape of the foot. If the arch is pushed upward by stretching, the rest of the sole is able to maintain its correct shape. The easiest way to stretch the arch is to grasp the sole at the toe and heel with the arch area facing you. Then, with the thumbs of both hands, push up on the arch while making an effort to keep the rest of the sole unchanged. When the arch is as high as you want it, match the sole to its pattern to make sure the shape is right. Actually the arch should be made just slightly higher than the desired height in order to compensate for natural give. After thumb molding I place the arch in my arch block and hammer it with a ball peen hammer to compress and stiffen the fibers. An arch block is simply a block of wood which has been shaped by carving or by burning and scraping to approximate the inverted arch of a foot. To protect the wood and preserve the shape of the arch indentation, the block should be covered with a piece of durable leather. (Notice the arch block in the collection of George Reeves's work.) First I mark the center line and edges of the arch with my thumbnail, comparing it to the original pattern. I start the hammering on these lines and then fill in the rest of the arch. Prestretched topsole leather is harder to mold, but it makes an arch that can't be beat. The opposing stresses resulting from the lamination create an arch that cannot easily be forced down. Before any further work can be done the soles must dry thoroughly. They will dry within a few hours if set in the sun; indoors it may take a couple of days. Now there should be two topsoles (left and right), two bottom soles, and a set of straps. The bottom soles have molded arches; the topsoles have molded arches and strap slots. The idea is to put them all together. The straps will be attached to the topsole and then the bottom sole will be glued and nailed on.

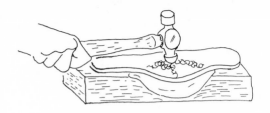

Hammering the arch on an arch block

First the soles must be prepared for the glue. Theoretically all loose fibers should be removed from the flesh side with a rasp. On most soling leather, however, the process of rasping off loose fibers merely exposes new fibers just as loose. All we can do is to maintain a uniformly roughened surface. One indication of high-quality soling is the absence of excessively loose fibers. The flesh side is generally plated so that it appears smooth and tight, but it can be easily tested for loose fibers by scraping it with your fingernail. Compare the tightness of fiber in cowhide and in horsehide. Horsehide is much tighter; unfortunately it is rarely available in suitable weights for bottom soles, but excellent topsole weights can be obtained.

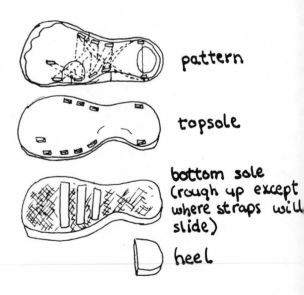

pattern

topsole

bottom sole (rough up except where straps will slide)

heel

Anyhow, either with a shoe rasp, sole rougher, or with a power sander, the flesh sides of the soles are roughened. If I am using continuous straps I may choose to avoid the areas where the straps pass under the topsole to allow the straps to slide more freely.

When I attach the straps I skive the ends carefully to eliminate bulk. Any lumps under the foot will cause the bottom sole to wear out that much faster. The skiving is always done from the flesh side to retain as much strength as possible. A dab of shoe cement is applied to both the strap and the sole.

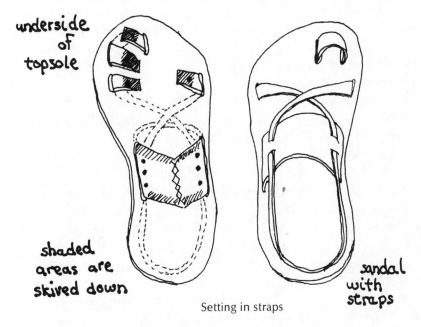

underside of topsole

shaded areas are skived down

Setting in straps

sandal with straps

When the cement is tacky, the strap is pressed down and fixed with a 1-ounce flathead shoe tack set in from the bottom and clinched on an anvil. Straps which come out at an angle should be set in at the same angle. If an angled strap is set in straight it will twist and rub on the foot uncomfortably. A good way to demonstrate this is to simply wrap a strap around your own foot in various ways and observe its behavior in different positions. Twisting is unavoidable in some places; straps must be broken in by the wearer in these spots. I lace all sliding straps and heel straps before gluing.

Glue should never be applied to straps intended to slide (on continuous-strap styles). Fixed straps and open areas should be well covered with glue. For added strength, a second coat of glue may be applied when the first coat has dried. Before putting the two soles together I cover sliding straps lightly with talcum powder to keep them from sticking to the bottom sole.

I put the soles together starting at the toe, then at the heel. Then I press the edges together, starting at the arch, following with the outside edge. Only after the edges are together do I press the inside areas. This insures that the dimensions remain constant. Ah, constancy! The arch is also made more accurate by this method. It is very important to press the edges securely. I do this by inverting the sandal and laying the edge on an anvil. Then, moving the sandal as I go, I hammer all around the edge, always keeping the anvil underneath the section I'm hammering. I pound the rest of the sandal from the top with a rubber mallet. After pounding the soles together, I pull any sliding straps back and forth to make sure they move freely.

Sandals with fixed strap designs require a preliminary fitting before gluing the soles. With the foot in the sandal I pull the straps snug and position them so they don't chafe the foot. I then glue and tack them to the topsole by placing the tacks close to the inside edge of the strap slot. Skive off excess leather with a slanting cut so that the end of the strap is flush with the sole. If the strap is very wide I sometimes sew the ends together underneath the topsole and skive the edges to reduce bulk. Sewing the ends of a wide strap to form a continuous loop eliminates the considerable stress on the tacks holding the strap in place. Some sandalmakers bring the straps out from between the soles so that they extend beyond the edges. This way they can tighten the straps, nail them at the outside edge of the strap slot, and cut off the excess leather after the soles are put together. Thus they avoid the preliminary fitting. I do not use this method because I believe the straps should follow the curve of the foot and also because it

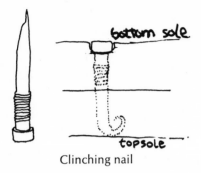

bottom sole

topsole

Clinching nail

shifts the stresses to the weakest part of the sandal — the edges.

Now the nailing begins. Shoe nails are made with specially designed shanks which curl around and clinch the leather when the points hit the anvil. This is why they are called clinching nails. The size of the nail depends on the thickness of the sole. The nail should be just long enough to allow the point to clinch (⅜ to ⅝ nails are suitable for typical soles). The tip of the nail is extremely sharp and tapered to one side. This gives it a slight directional quality which guides the nail at a little bit of an angle. This quality can be used to direct the nails away from straps (so the strap can slide freely), away from edges (so the nails won't protrude), and, to top it off, if a nail goes in crooked and is removed, the point of a second nail can be inserted into the hole of the original nail pointing away from the bend; the point will bite into the edge of the hole and guide the nail straight, rather than follow the original hole. Clinching nails are always set in from the bottom of the sandal. If they are put in from the top, the clinch will wear down until it breaks and the head of the nail will be pushed up into someone's foot. Some people are under the impression that the points will be pushed up into the foot if the nails are inserted from the bottom, but this is not so. The ridges as well as the taper of the shank hold the nail in place; the head merely wears away along with the sole.

To put a nail in next to a strap to anchor the topsole in this area of particularly high stress, I use the nail to sight along the edge of the sandal. When I am satisfied with its position in relation to the strap, I slide the nail down the edge of the soles and insert the point about ¼ inch in. The sandal is placed upside down on the anvil and the nail struck sharply with the hammer. It should be struck just once, hard enough to put it straight through and make it clinch. Hitting the nail more than once tends to make it bend. I firmly believe in the "one toke, one stroke" nailing method. I space nails about one to an inch. More than this is unnecessary and merely makes inaccuracies in your work more conspicuous. The arch can be strengthened by setting nails around and within it, being careful not to nail through any sliding straps. As a guide, I make lines in the leather with my thumbnail on either side of the strap I want to avoid. Anywhere on these lines (or in the area between two adjacent straps) is safe for nailing. Ordinarily I end up with about five or six nails on the inside of the arch and two or three nails within the arch itself.

I don't know why I wait until this point to cut out the heels. It would probably be easier to cut them with the soles. Nevertheless, this is my usual procedure. (Everyone is allowed certain illogical moves, I suppose.) The most important criterion in

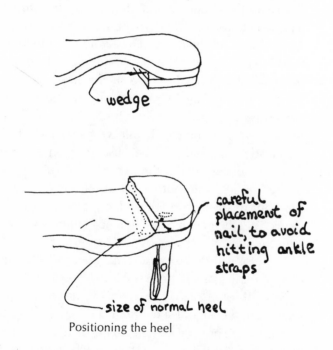

Positioning the heel

cutting heel patterns is to make sure that the length of the heel permits the front or breast edge to be nailed easily without being obstructed by heel straps and strap slots. At the same time, make sure the heel does not extend into the arch area. If the arch is too close to the heel, it will be practically impossible to make the heel fit all these specifications. If the heel is long enough to nail the breast edge in front of the heel straps, it will project into the arch; if it is short enough to leave the breast edge behind the arch, you will find yourself nailing directly into the ankle strap. There are two solutions: make a wedge where the heel extends into the arch; or nail expertly between the ankle strap slot and the edge of the sole on the arch side, and angle the breast line of the heel so it ends in front of the ankle strap on the opposite side. In any case, the heel of the sandal must be large enough to provide a full platform under the ball of the heel. I generally mark the heel on the sole pattern simply by marking the position of the breast line on either side of the pattern with an awl. An awl hole is a good mark because it can be seen on both sides of the pattern, especially important when only one pattern is used. I mark the position of the breast line on the bottom sole through the awl holes on the pattern. Then I connect the two marks with a straightedge to produce a guideline for cutting. To mark the position of the breast line on the sole, I simply trace the breast edge of the cut heel. After the heel is cut, I rough up both the flesh side of the heel and the area of the sole behind the breast line. The heel will wear down and need to be removed and replaced repeatedly throughout the life of the sandal. Therefore, rather than bond it as tightly as I do the soles, with two coats of glue, I use only one coat of glue on the heel.

The sandal is ready for finishing when the soles and heels are all nailed together. Finishing involves sanding or rasping the edges, smoothing, dyeing, and burnishing the edges, fitting the straps, and attaching the heel and toe plates.

The traditional line finisher used by shoemakers and cobblers is the ideal machine for sanding sandal edges. It does rough, medium and fine sanding as well as buffing and polishing. It is also the most expensive device. The next most efficient machine is a belt sander. A decent belt sander is still expensive, and isn't as versatile as the line finisher. An inexpensive alternative is a small sanding drum designed for use on a drill press, which will fit on the shaft of an electric motor. The drum is available from some hardware suppliers, or from Sears, Roebuck, and a suitable electric motor can be found in almost any discarded refrigerator or in shops dealing in used tools. If you still can't afford it, smooth the edges with your rasp and finish it off by hand with, say, an 80-grit sandpaper (give or take a few grits). This is the method I have used for the last dozen or so pairs of sandals I have made. The finish can be just as fine this way as with power sanders. If you are using motorized sanding machines, take care to hold the sandal straps away from the sandpaper and moving parts of the machine. If you aren't careful, you will scratch up the straps. If the straps get caught in the machine it will ruin the sandals and you could get hurt as well. Even with a hand rasp you can scratch the straps if you are careless.

Finally the edges are beveled, then dyed and burnished. Edge dye is suitable for this. A wax such as Propert's Shoe Cream applied over the dye will really put a shine on the edges. I used to make a mixture of leather dye, antique dye, edge dye, and leather balm. I got an excellent edge finish by this mixing process, the effectiveness of which improved when it was left to stand in an open jar for several days or weeks. Some mixtures worked better than others, but since I didn't take notes you'll have to experiment for yourself. The mixture should be thin enough to apply with a dauber.

To fit continuous sliding straps I first powder the foot with talc and make sure the straps are loose enough to allow the foot to slide into the sandal easily. With the foot in the sandal, tighten the straps, working from the fixed ends toward the free ends. The straps should be snug but not tight. When the straps are tightened I mark the buckle location with my thumbnail on both strap ends. The proper location for the buckle is at the soft fleshy area in front of the outside ankle bone. A hole is punched at each mark, then extra holes are added for tightening to accommodate strap stretch. Foot swelling doesn't affect the placement of holes; any strap cut to a width of ¾ inch or less will stretch enough to accommodate swelling. As a matter of fact, with holes every ½ inch, the straps will sometimes stretch two to three holes in the first hour of wear. I feel that

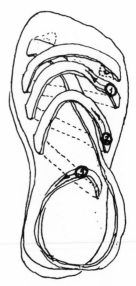

Tightening the straps

Conway buckle

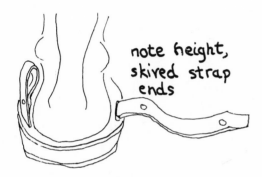

note height, skived strap ends

Positioning ankle straps

Heel plate

fewer holes are more pleasing aesthetically, so I use a Conway buckle, which is adjustable in both directions. I punch five holes in the front strap, each about ½ inch apart and two holes in the back strap about 1 or 1¼ inches apart. This gives an overall span of about 3 inches, which is usually adequate. It also allows the buckle to be kept in the most comfortable position, whether the straps stretch toward the front or the back.

The loops of the ankle strap must be made the proper size and height. The size of the loops must be large enough for the strap to pass through easily. I make them large enough to allow the buckle to pass through as well. This is unnecessary, but it's worth it, especially if you aren't using Conway buckles. The height of the ankle loops should be such that it keeps the strap which encircles the heel from rubbing on the ankle bones. This height is almost invariably equal to the width of the heel. This makes it possible to set the height without having the foot in the sandal. I often do this in advance of the final fitting to save time. I bend the straps down across the heel of the sandal and mark the height with my thumbnail where it crosses the opposite strap slot. I double each strap into a loop at this mark and punch a hole through both layers about 1 inch from where the strap emerges from the sole. With the hole at the free end as a starting point, I skive the end of the ankle strap to a feather edge. Skiving removes excess length at the same time. Then I truncate the corners of this feather edge for appearance. Skiving the ends makes the ankle straps much more comfortable as there is less protruding bulk to rub against the foot. A single small rivet is used to fasten the loop.

The final step that must be taken before the first step is taken is the addition of heel and toe plates. I use number 2 plates for the heels, double aught (00) for the toes. I prefer malleable steel plates with prongs and holes. Plastic plates are also available and are well recommended. Even with prongs, the plates must be nailed in to be sure they are secure. For this I use a suitable size clinching nail (usually ⅝ or ⅞). Occasionally the holes will be too small for the nail heads to pass through; if this happens the heads should be filed down flush with the plate so that the sandals won't injure floors and rugs. I find that the plates are usually best placed under the big toe and just off center toward the outside edge on the heel. However, I always look at how other footwear has been worn down by the same person before placing his or her heel and toe plates.

Now is the time to put the sandals on and walk in them. Since I make my straps from horsehide it is imperative that I stress the importance of their proper care. In view of this consideration, I have always supplied a can of mink oil, neat's-foot oil, Hubbard's Shoe Grease, or some other leather nutrient, as discussed earlier, and advise that it be applied to the straps after every few weeks of wearing. If this is not done the straps will eventually break where they emerge from the strap slots, especially the toe and ankle straps, which must bear a lot of stress.

Variations of course can and should be made on this procedure. Stitching or lacing instead of rivets may be used to fasten the ankle straps. Straps may be left long and tapered at the ends for tying, rather than using a buckle. Other buckleless designs are also possible.

High-heeled sandals present uniquely different problems. For one thing, the entire area of the arch is eliminated and replaced by a steel shank in the adjacent area of the sole known as the waist. The heel must be angled to correspond to its height, higher heels being more sharply angled. The curve of the shank must also correspond to the height. Extremely high heels are totally impractical for sandals, as the foot tends to slide forward uncontrollably; the higher the heel, the more problems there will be with slipping. In all high-heeled sandals the straps must be designed very carefully to keep the foot from slipping, and a slightly larger border should be added to the toe. A reasonable height is 1¼ to 2 inches. Unfinished wooden heels of this height range with corresponding shanks are available from leather and shoe supply dealers. They are made in various widths to accommodate different-size feet. They can be dyed to match the sandals. If wooden heels of this type are used, the seat (the area of the sole corresponding to the heel) must be cut according to the shape of the heel rather than to the shape of the foot. I make up stacked leather heels by laminating blocks of sole leather ten layers thick, 2½ inches wide, and as long as the leather I am using allows. This is a very tedious task, as each surface must be roughed up to prepare for gluing, and the glue can only be applied to one side at a time. This means that to glue up ten layers one has to glue five pairs of single layers, then two pairs of double layers (one double-layer strip left over), then one quadruple-layered pair, then the resulting eight-layered slab with the leftover double-layer strip. Thus there are twenty surfaces to be prepared and four separate gluing operations. If it takes only fifteen minutes for the glue to dry after each application and one minute for each surface to be roughed up, the overall time will be an hour and twenty minutes just for laminating the leather. Because of this time expenditure, I find it worthwhile to make a lot at once. It takes very little extra time to laminate two or three times as much, and laminated heel stacks remain usable indefinitely. For making larger quantities it is best to double or triple the width of each layer and simply cut the laminated slabs into 2½-inch strips. An added advantage of this method is that it provides at least one smooth edge. If the strip is from the center of a triple-width slab, both the breast edge and the back edge will be smooth. Also, if you don't have a bandsaw, you will have to find someone who has one and is willing either to let you use it or else to cut the heels for you. Under these circumstances, I think it would be wise to cut as many heels at one time as you can afford.

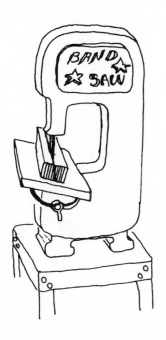

The laminated stack is cut obliquely across the center two layers. This cannot be done easily except by using a bandsaw, with the work platform pivoted to an angle to make the oblique cut. The result is two continuous-width heel strips, complete with the appropriate angle for the height of a heel of this many laminations. The individual heels are most easily cut out on the bandsaw, but they can also be cut out with a jigsaw or (as a last resort) even with a shoe knife. As with a simple one-layer heel, the breast line is marked on the sandal pattern with awl holes. The breast line is then lined up with the front edge of the heel stack strip and the outline of the heel is marked on the leather. The pattern must be reversed for left and right heels. The breast line is also marked on the bottom sole, and the area behind the line is rasped for gluing. If the breast edge is to be finished, it should be done before attaching the heel to the sole.

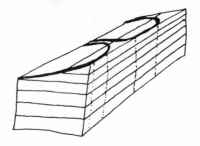

Laminated heel stack

The stress on high heels is tremendous, such that they are prone to be torn from the soles at every step. This stress makes a sturdy fastening imperative. I have found that threaded masonry nails are the most effective fastening device available. Once these nails are in, the heels cannot be removed. They are driven in from the flesh side of the bottom soles through the heel. On leather stack heels I also drive a couple in from the bottom of the heel near the back edge to secure the lamination. The one big drawback is that the shortest of these nails available is 1¼ inches long. The stack heel I have just described usually comes out a fraction of an inch shorter than that at the breast edge. Because these nails are made of hardened steel they can gouge an anvil and ruin its smooth surface. If there is any possibility of this happening, put an extra layer of leather between the heel and anvil to protect its surface. Protruding nail points can be filed or sanded flush with the bottom of the heel if desired, but this is not really necessary since they will be covered by another layer, the toplift.

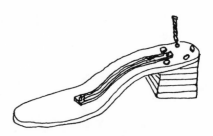

Fastening heel to bottom sole

The toplift is the replaceable layer added to the bottom of the heel that bears the brunt of road abrasion. The toplift is attached with ordinary shoe nails (long sizes are preferable) so that it can be removed easily for replacement.

The steel shank is placed with the flat end at the heel and the bent end toward the ball of the foot. The curve of the shank should correspond to the curve of the foot's arch. A medium-size (⅜-inch or 2-oz.) shoe tack is used to nail the shank to the heel. The sole is then curved to conform to the shank and the front end of the shank is nailed to the sole with a short (⅜-inch or 1½-oz.) clinching tack. In order to prevent resistance to sliding straps, I glue a strip of thin (1-to-2-oz.) leather over the shank.

The high heel becomes a difficult obstacle to work with when nailing the soles together. A narrow French hammer is used to set nails in close to the heel. Clinching nails are unsuitable for the heel seat; instead, special heel nails are used that, like the masonry nails, have a spiral thread to keep them from working loose.

Aside from the addition of the shank and heel and the absence of the arch area, the construction techniques are basically the same for high-heeled and molded arch sandals. On high-heeled sandals, however, I tend to make the topsole out of slightly lighter-weight material. The shank frees the topsole from its role as workhorse, supporting the arch. Therefore I prefer to make a more delicate, refined sandal using a lighter topsole.

One summer John and Gene came to work with me, two of my finest apprentices. They came practically at the same time the sandal season began, and there was quite a bit of work to be done. Neither John nor Gene had ever made sandals before, so, after explaining the basic process, I set both of them to work making pairs of sandals for themselves, for one another, and for me. The only requirement I set was that each pair should be a different style. These six pairs of sandals were made over the span of about a week. During that time they also performed simple operations such as preparing straps for customer orders. At the end of the week we had six samples in use, and both John and Gene had become competent sandalmakers. I turned all the sandalmaking operations over to them directly. Although people like Zebo Starker and Dick Whelan, who have been making sandals for many, many years, might object to my saying it, I believe that with such basic practice anyone can become quite proficient.

The technique of braiding, plaiting, and knotting leather strands is at once a very primitive and most sophisticated way of manipulating the material. It is a different world. The aesthetic appeal of a well-finished piece of knotwork or braiding is prodigious. The amount of time and patience involved is considerable. I can't possibly go into more than the most simple braids. For anyone interested by my humble introduction, there is a superb book which covers completely every aspect of the subject, *The Encyclopedia of Rawhide and Leather*

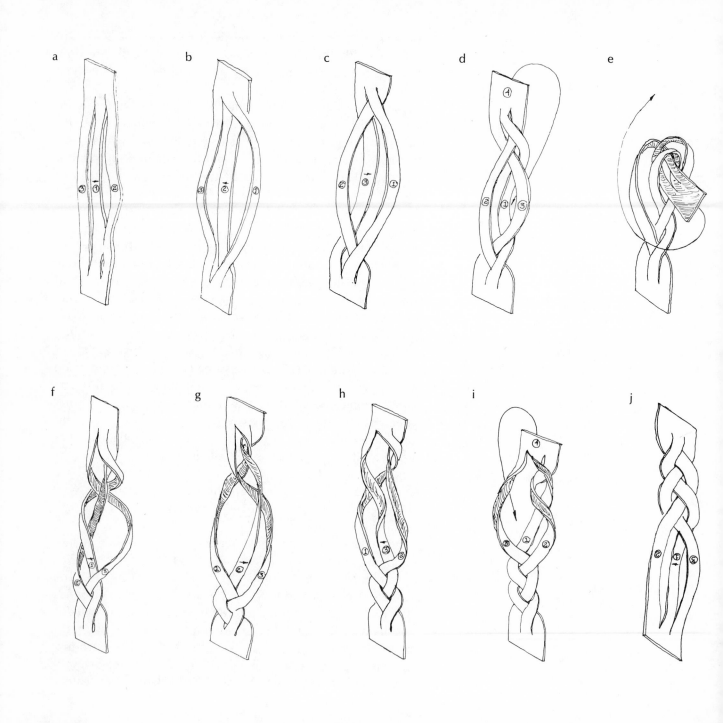

Braiding, by Bruce Grant, published by the Cornell Maritime Press in Cambridge, Maryland.

One of the simplest braids is the three-strand solid braid, also called a mystery braid. The name "solid braid" refers to the fact that instead of being made from three narrow strands it is made from *one* wide strap the ends of which are not cut. The braid will not remain a mystery to you if you read on and pay attention to the drawings.

For the first step, as in familiar open-end braiding (every girl's pigtails), the center strand is passed over to the outside; the former outside strand becomes the new center. This procedure is repeated, alternating the passes from left to right. After every third pass the far end of the braid is pulled through from the bottom between the newly positioned outside and center strands. The full sequence is six passes — this never varies — divided into two three-pass segments. When the braid is completed, it can be easily redistributed to close up gaps.

This type of braid is ideal for belts, straps for bags, and wristbands. Belts may require six full sequences; wristbands require only one. To achieve a smooth, even result it is important to use the right weight leather. The optimum weight depends on the width of the strands. For best results I use 6-ounce leather for braids with ⅜-inch strands, 8-ounce leather for braids with ½-inch strands, and 9-ounce leather for braids with ⅝-inch strands. Solid braids look best when each strand is neatly beveled on the grain side or the side that shows. Use a small brush to apply edge dye to the ends of slits between the strands. Always dye the ends of the slits from the back side in order to avoid getting any dye on the front of the braid. The completed braid should be laid flat by pulling the strap back and forth over a smooth round pole or other suitable object. This should be done on both the flesh side and the grain side in order to smooth and flatten the braid.

A five-strand solid braid is done in the same way. However, with five strands, the center strand must pass over two outside strands. A full sequence is two five-pass segments. After every fifth pass the far end of the strap is pulled through the braid from beneath between the newly positioned outside strand and the strand adjacent.

Once you have done a five-strand braid, you will not need to be told how to do seven, nine, or eleven strands. But, remember, the more strands the braid has the ropier it will be. Also, more strands or a tighter braid will shorten the finished length of the strap.

A rope is many things to me. Ropes are tools used for holding things together, up, down, open, and closed, for pulling, lifting, and lowering. Ropes are experiences — climbing, hauling, tying, swinging. I think of the threads I use for sewing as the tiny ropes that hold my world together. Ropes are textures, both visual and tactile. Braided leather ropes made from elk or moose hide with the soft flesh side exposed have the most sensuous texture. On the other hand, a rope made from a 5-ounce oil-and-chrome-tanned cowhide is the image of toughness. If made from tapered strands, it becomes fierce as a whip.

The four-strand round braid is made by bringing the outside strand under the two adjacent strands, and then back over the second of these two strands. This procedure is repeated, alternating from the right to left sides. The strands may be held in a clamp or attached to any object by means of bleed knots. I start ropes on rings, which are useful for attaching the finished ropes to ceilings, walls and limbs of trees. Care must be taken to see that the strands follow the contour of the braid without twisting. The basic procedure for round braids is: under all but one strand, then back over half of these to a position right or left of center. Thus, for four strands the procedure is: under two, over one; for six strands, under four, over two; for eight strands, under six, over three, etc. Because of the tubular form of this braid, the weight of the leather must be appropriately chosen according to the width of the strands in order to give it the necessary rigidity so that it won't flatten out too easily — I leave this judgment to you.

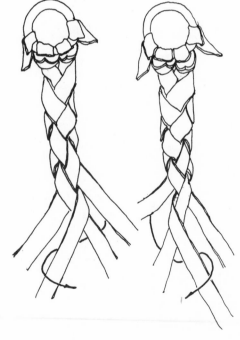

Round braid pattern

Garment Leather

Garment leathers can be sewn, laced, glued, braided, folded, and knotted to create finished articles. Most of these techniques should be relatively familiar to you by now as techniques used for heavier leathers. There are minor differences (garment leather is not rasped or sanded before gluing, sewing holes need not be prepunched, strips of garment leather are folded or rolled lengthwise to give them sufficient bulk for knotting), but the techniques remain basically the same. The techniques of sewing, however, become much more elaborate with the use of a sewing machine.

A sewing machine is clearly unsurpassed for efficiency in sewing garment leather. Certain machines are specially designed, and thus better suited, for stitching leather. However, almost any sewing machine can be made to serve the purpose effectively until you have the desire or wherewithal to upgrade your equipment with a more efficient machine. If you do not have a suitable machine and are planning to purchase one, get one that will be adequate for the work you will be doing. Conventional home sewing machines can be used to sew light garment leathers and simple pieces made of heavier leathers. Heavy-duty industrial machines accommodate a broader range of weights in the materials they can sew. An industrial machine with a needle feed provides a very accurate stitch for all garment work. Adding a walking foot produces a compound feed machine that delivers a constant stitch length even on fairly heavy leathers (an average compound feed machine can handle seams up to ½ inch thick). A 29-series, treadle-drive cobbler's machine is good for shoe and bag work because of the boot-arm workbed which allows it to sew in hard-to-reach areas. By fitting it with a removable table, it can also be used for garment work, but it takes skill to guide the material along accurately due to its inefficient feed mechanism. Compound-feed cylinder arm and post machines are also available for positive stitch control on specialized applications. Post machines, for instance, are superb for topstitching the seams on trouser legs. In gen-

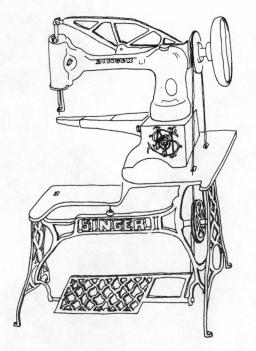

Treadle drive sewing machine

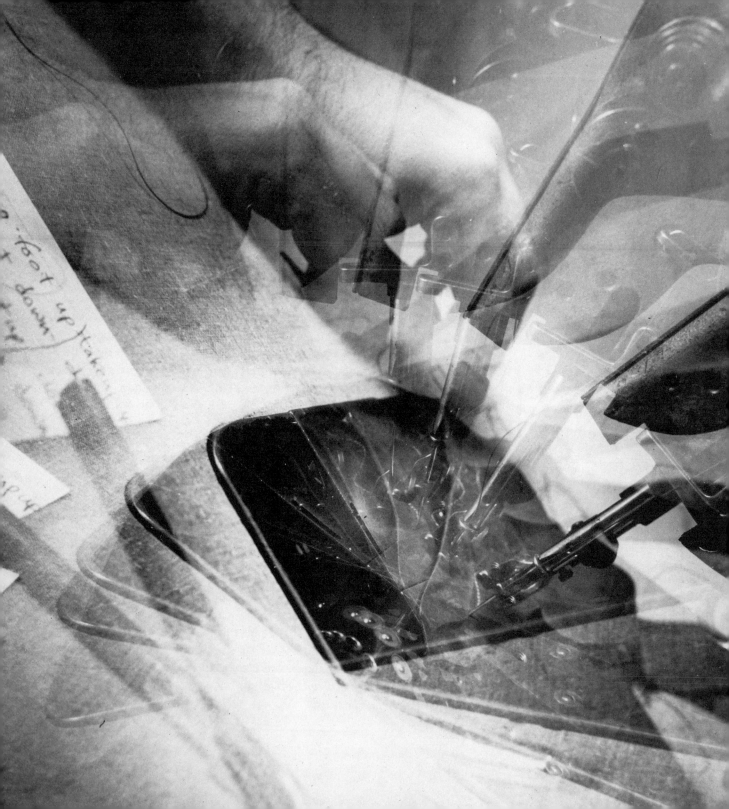

eral, however, an ordinary flat bed machine is usually most suitable.

To understand why certain machines are better for leatherwork, examine the various feed mechanisms. Standard cloth machines move the material along with the feed dog, a toothed device which moves back and forth under the presser foot, receding beneath the slotted feed dog plate on the forward stroke. Thus the material is moved only on the back stroke.

The presser foot's most important function is to hold the material down while the thread loop is forming (see page 120). But it also must keep the material from shifting during the rest of the stitch procedure. Thus, it always creates a certain amount of resistance to the movement of the material. The presser foot can be lifted manually to position the material for stitching. The upper tension spring is linked to the presser foot lift so that the thread tension is released when the foot is raised. On industrial machines the presser foot lift is coupled to either a treadle or knee lifter. These allow much more efficient operation as they leave both hands free. The knee lifter is best, but care must be taken not to lift the presser foot accidentally with the knee while sewing. Otherwise the thread loop will not form properly and may jam in the hook assembly. Because of the drag created by the presser foot, the feed dog alone is not sufficient for moving along heavier materials such as leather smoothly and evenly.

If you are stuck with this type of feed mechanism, there are two things you can do to alleviate the problem. First, ease the spring tension on the presser foot. This will reduce drag but will require more careful guiding of the material. Too little tension will create the same problems as accidental lifting of the presser foot. To compensate for this, a slightly thinner needle and thread or a specially designed leather needle may be used. Also, a light dusting of talcum powder will allow the material to slide more easily. On heavy-duty machines designed for leather and other heavy materials, the problem is solved with rolling presser feet or with additional feed mechanisms.

On cloth machines the needle moves straight up and down. The material can only move when the needle is in a raised position. On needle-feed machines the needle's timing is reversed and it is given an additional back-and-forth motion that is simultaneous with that of the feed dog. The material moves when the needle is in the lowered position, piercing and pulling it along. This is a very smooth mechanism which produces an extremely even stitch length. On walking foot machines an extra foot known as the work foot moves simultaneously with the feed dog in a clamping motion to move the material along. This mechanism can handle uneven thicknesses of material more easily than the needle feed, but it does not have as smooth an action. On compound feed machines the walking foot and needle feed are both employed, creating superior material handling characteristics.

If you plan to buy a sewing machine, keep your eye out for the auctions of a defunct shoe factory; it may be well worth your while to attend. If you find a machine that meets your requirements and you have enough cash to make the high bid, you may get a real bargain. Because of the constant wear that factory machines are subjected to, it is important to check out the condition of the machine before bidding. Make sure that it stitches properly and that all the parts move freely without too much play (loose movements are an indication of excessive wear). Some consideration should be given to the table and motor as well. A motor with a built-in clutch is preferable to one with a separate clutch assembly because the action is smoother and quieter. A heavy, solid wood table with a sturdy stand reduces vibration and is more pleasing to the eye than a Formica table. Factories often use a common table for a group of machines. If the machine you want is part of such a group, the table and motor will have to be acquired separately. Machines with missing, broken, or worn-out parts should be left for the dealer to repair.

If you buy your machine from a dealer you have a right to expect it to sew perfectly. You will have the security of knowing exactly what you are getting and the assurance that it will work properly. For many people this assurance is worth the extra cost. Also, when buying from a dealer you have the opportunity to compare the advantages of various feed mechanisms as well as such features as oversized bobbins, reversing mechanisms, and specialized (post or cylinder arm) workbeds.

Even if your sewing machine is in perfect condition when you first get it, there are a number of problems that will probably arise sooner or later. Most of these problems can be corrected easily. Some are more difficult, but rarely should your machine require the bothersome services of a repair shop. The only tools you will need to care for your machine properly are a can of stainless sewing machine oil, a lint brush, a good pair of tweezers, a set of screwdrivers, and, rarely, an extra-fine-grade slipstone or waterproof sandpaper.

The sewing machine should be lubricated at every oiling point before each day's use. Stainless oil (obtained through a sewing machine dealer) is best; oil spots picked up by the leather need not cause panic as they will fade in a short time. After lubrication, the machine should be wiped free of excess oil with an absorbent deerskin or chamois rag. The bobbin race must be lubricated more frequently since it is an area of close tolerances where smooth, free movement is essential. As a rule, the bobbin race and hook movements should be oiled every time the bobbin is changed, more often when necessary. Industrial machines are often fitted with thread oilers, as maximum stitch tension can only be achieved with lubricated threads. The bobbin thread can be oiled if necessary through the holes on the sides of the bobbin (this is necessary only with extremely stiff or heavy threads). Various silicone compounds have been developed especially for thread lubrication, but I have found that stainless oil works well enough without the objectionable odor of the silicone compounds.

A small brush and a good pair of tweezers are necessary for removing bits of snagged thread and accumulated lint, both of which inhibit free movement of the bobbin and hook assemblies. I find that snags occur with annoying frequency (usually an indication of inadequate lubrication); I feel this warrants a handy location for tweezers. I keep mine stuck in the middle hole of the triple-hole thread guide located just above the upper tension spring; I skip this hole when looping thread through the guide.

There are many instances where screwdrivers are needed. Broken or mashed screwdrivers are frustratingly useless, so don't cheat yourself with cheap ersatz. Invest in a set of good-quality screwdrivers. They will pay off in the long run. (Those made by Snap-On Tools for auto mechanics are indestructable.) A medium-size screwdriver with a ¼-inch head is used when changing presser feet for special applications. It is also used for changing needles to accommodate varying thread sizes, to change point styles, or simply when the old needle is dull, bent, or broken.

Sewing machine needles have a groove running down the shank to the needle eye. The thread runs down this groove and through the eye. The groove allows the thread to move freely on that side of the needle when the needle has been inserted into the material. This is important in order for the thread to form a loop which the hook will carry around the bobbin thread, and then to allow the take-up arm (located above the needle on the machine head) to pull the loop tight, locking the stitch. On the side of the needle opposite the groove there is a depression, just above the needle eye, where the bobbin hook catches the loop. It must be in the proper position for the loop to be caught consistently. If the needle is inserted sideways or backward, or simply not inserted completely, the hook will not catch the loop. Of course the needle must be the proper size. The shank length and diamete depend on the machine itself, according to the size of the needle bar, etc. The size of the eye, on the other hand, must be chosen to correspond to the size of the thread. If the eye is too large the thread will tend to jump around erratically within the eye and fray. If the eye is too small the thread will not fit through easily; if forced through it will also fray. For a #99 nylon thread I generally use a size 20 eye, although one step in either direction makes little difference. I ordinarily use round (or "cloth") point needles. For particularly tough leather, several special point styles are available: diamond points, wedge and narrow wedge points, left and right twist points, and cross points. I like the narrow wedge points, but I suggest that you experiment to determine your own preferences. Because of the high speeds involved, sewing machine needles require more polishing than hand needles. I have been told that there are over twenty polishing operations in the production of the finest sewing machine needles. Even the best needles, however, exhibit signs of wear after prolonged use. Roughness around the eye that can fray the thread or bluntness of the point indicate that the needle should be changed.

Occasionally it is necessary to delve deeper into the inner workings of the machine. For these occasions I find a longer shank screwdriver essential for greater torque and easier manipulation; an 8-inch-shank length is the minimum. For general work, three head sizes are required: $\frac{1}{8}$, $\frac{5}{32}$, and $\frac{7}{32}$ inch. These are used to adjust the position of the oscillating arm (which allows the loop to slip by obstructions around the bobbin basket), the hook (which catches the loop and pulls it around the bobbin basket), and the needle bar (which controls the alignment of the needle and the hook; from its lowest position, the needle must rise a short distance, forming a loop in the thread, and meet the hook at the depression just above the needle eye, where the loop is caught by the hook). Screwdrivers are also used to remove the feed dog and feed dog plate for access to the bobbin and hook assembly. In the case of severe tangles and jamming, the entire bobbin assembly must be taken out and freed of obstructions. A miniature screwdriver with a $\frac{3}{32}$-inch head is used to remove the bobbin basket retainer plate; then, with the hook positioned at eleven o'clock, the bobbin basket is easily lifted out.

Damage or excessive wear to the hook is rare, and is usually associated with other problems, such as loose screws and bent or broken needles. A damaged or dull hook will not catch the thread loop properly, and thus causes stitch failure. Careful honing with a fine India or Arkansas slipstone (or waterproof sandpaper) followed with crocus cloth may correct the problem. Repeated damage to the hook will, however, require its replacement.

If such repair operations leave you undismayed, you may want to disassemble the hook shaft and other assemblies in order to increase your understanding of the machine. As with any puzzle, allow yourself ample time for proper reassembly. If you proceed carefully and patiently, you will soon be able to take care of any problem that may arise. Of course, many problems (even broken needles and tangled threads) begin to disappear as you become more experienced in handling the machine. The only way to acquire this experience is through continuous persistent work. The following few paragraphs contain suggestions which should help you to use your sewing machine with optimum efficiency.

One of the most frustrating problems when sewing with an industrial machine is French knotting, snags which occur on the first few stitches of a seam. French knots eliminate the possibility of a neat tie-off, and sometimes continue farther into the seam, causing a weak, loose stitch. There is, however, a simple way to protect against this problem. Most sewing manuals merely tell you to begin stitching with the loose ends of both threads pulled toward the back of the machine. This is important since it keeps the loop from twisting, but it is not enough; it doesn't eliminate French knotting. French knots are caused by excessive slack on the first stitch that the take-up arm is unable to eliminate. Therefore this excess slack must be removed manually. After the needle has been inserted into the material, when the take-up arm is at its lowest position, release the upper tension by raising the presser foot (with the knee or treadle lifter), and pull the thread from the guide just above the upper tension spring. This removes the excess slack from the take-up arm. Now lower the presser foot and continue stitching. French knots occurring in the middle of a seam indicate accidental lifting of the presser foot and consequent release of tension, or severe misadjustment of the tension.

To achieve a regular stitch, a balance must be maintained between the upper and lower tensions. I keep the bobbin spring tightened completely for maximum tension, and adjust the balance with the top tension spring. If the tension on the top thread is too tight, the lower, or bobbin, thread will be pulled through, forming a loop on top of the seam. This causes puckering and weakens the seam. If the tension on the top thread is too loose, the thread will be pulled down, forming a loop on the bottom of the seam which can tangle and jam in the bobbin assembly. The tension balance can be easily checked and adjusted in the first few stitches; it should remain consistent as the same thread and material are used. If the thread twists as it passes through the tension device, the stitch will "pop"; the tension on one stitch will be too tight and on the next too loose. This results from using poor-quality thread, or thread with a reverse twist. Reverse twist threads are made for use only on the left-hand needle of double needle machines. Thread with knots in it should be discarded to protect the sewing machine as well as your work. Many leathers exert a strong effect on the tension; because of this I have found it necessary to fit the upper tension device with a heavy-duty spring to minimize fluctuations.

Several hand tools are used with the sewing machine. The drawers commonly attached to sewing machine tables are generally much too small and inconvenient to store more than a few of these tools. In my drawer, for instance, I keep only a lint brush, two small screwdrivers, a box of matches, and an assortment of needles. Fortunately, the sewing machine itself provides ample opportunity for improvising suitable and handy tool locations.

A blunt awl comes into frequent use at the sewing machine. For removing seams it is superior to conventional seam rippers, which not only leave numerous hard-to-remove loops of thread, but all too often nick and cut the leather. With practice, the awl can be used to pick stitches quickly and efficiently. It is sometimes necessary to remove seams stitch by stitch, but it is often possible to remove two or three stitches at a time, especially if the tension of the thread is tighter on one side than on the other (in this case the stitches are pulled from the tighter side). As the thread is pulled out of the seam, the end sometimes begins to ravel; when this happens, the thread should be snipped to avoid snags. My awl has made itself at home in a deep oil hole at the right-hand side of the sewing machine head, where I automatically reach for it when occasion calls. (I wipe the hole with a Q-Tip after oiling, to keep the awl dry.)

Nylon thread should always be tied off and melted at the ends of seams. Bring both threads to the back of the seam by pulling on the lower thread until the top thread is drawn through in a loop, then pull the end through with the awl. Tie a square knot, then snip the ends short and melt the knot. Tie-offs should be kept to a minimum. In many cases, seams can be stitched so that they end in the same hole they began in (e.g., the seam around the edge of a hat brim). Then both ends can be tied off at the same time. Be sure to pull the starting threads to the back of the seam before making the last few stitches. This will insure against tangling that can make it impossible to pull the thread through. When the seam is complete, the final thread can be pulled through and the knot tied with paired threads. Tie-offs should be made in an inconspicuous spot (such as at a cross seam) or on the inside of the piece. Fused nylon can be uncomfortably scratchy, so tie-offs should not be made in areas that will be in close contact with the skin. I keep a box of Ohio Blue Tip matches in front of the sewing machine drawer for melting knots. I cut the striker plate from the matchbox and glue it to the table in a convenient spot for easy striking and I keep an ashtray nearby for used matches. If there are several tie-offs on a piece, I melt them all at once. This conserves matches; with practice, as many as ten knots can be melted with one match.

Thread snips are much more efficient than regular scissors for snipping threads. Plastic snips with replaceable blades may look and feel nice, but compared with good-quality, solid metal snips they are worthless. With good snips the biggest problem is the rattle. Since the natural place for a pair of snips to be is on a vibrating sewing machine table, I have found that gluing a pad of soft leather to the area of the table where the snips usually lie is the only way to keep them quiet. Now, about snipped threads — they cling to carpets and other rough floor surfaces and they tangle in broom bristles when sweeping them from smooth floors. The best way to avoid the nuisance of cleaning up these pesky snippings is to collect them before they get away. Accumulated snippings are ideal for stuffing pillows (about one medium-sized pillow every three years) or, if you can't wait that long, leather animals and dolls (one small animal every few months). I keep a bucket for snippings at the side of my machine. When I snip threads I hold them in my left hand, with the snippers in my right hand, and simply drop the snipped threads in the bucket as I snip them. (My left-handed friends do it the other way around.)

There are occasions when a pair of shears is also useful at the machine, such as for clipping curved seams and trimming seam allowances (as well as for those times when the thread snips mysteriously disappear until you stand up and find that you've been sitting on them). Taped seams and other seams in areas of low stress are often trimmed close to the stitching by sliding the shears alongside the seam with the points close together while pulling gently on the strip being removed. This technique is especially important for taped seams, as the tape is sewn on from the back, and wide seam allowances must be used to insure adequate coverage. Trimming should always be done before crossing the seam with further stitching. Seam trimmings may be collected either with or separately from thread snippings, and in the same manner. To be sure, shears rattle even worse than snips. I keep my shears hung, with my long screwdrivers, off to one side of the table in an open pouch, where they are not affected by vibrations.

The flat plate alongside the hand wheel at the top of the machine is an ideal spot for a small magnet. It can be used to hold loose needles, special presser feet, seam guides, and other small parts. Under the table are several jutting bolts which can be used to store such tools as a mallet and a deerskin rag. The mallet is used for flattening lumpy seams to facilitate stitching over them. The rag is for wiping excess oil from the machine after its daily lubrication. Deerskin (or chamois) makes the best oil rags because of its suppleness and high absorbency. The oil can is kept on its own absorbent pad on the floor next to the thread bucket. The type with a thin, flexible spout is best.

When sewing near obstacles (such as lumpy seams, snaps, etc.), you can come closer than otherwise possible by moving the material sideways. To do this lift the presser foot when the needle is well out of the material, then bring the needle down close to the material, positioning it over the proper point. Then lower the presser foot and continue the stitch cycle. As long as the presser foot is raised only with the needle out of the material, the tension will not be affected.

When sewing tight curves or angles (as in decorative topstitching), the material must be moved with the needle piercing it. The needle is inserted only a short way, the machine is stopped, the presser foot is raised, and the material positioned for the new stitch direction. The presser foot is then lowered and the stitch cycle continued. When changing the direction of the stitch in this way, all sewing machine action must stop while the presser foot is raised, to avoid fouling the thread. When doing decorative topstitching, I mark the design with the awl, either freehand or with a template. The awl is best for this as it leaves no visible marks under the stitching.

Easing is simply the technique of sewing together two pieces of material with unequal seam lengths between aligned end points, thus imparting a slight pucker to the longer side of the seam. This is done either purely for appearance or in order to allow more freedom of movement in certain areas of garments (such as around armholes and across the back). Contrary to the suggestions of most sewing manuals, seams can be eased without elaborate basting. Make sure that both the starting and end points are aligned properly, with the shorter side of the seam on the bottom. Hold the end points together with the right hand (or the left if you are left-handed), keeping an easy tension on the seam. While stitching the seam, the fingers of the other hand precede the needle in a sort of spiderlike walking motion which gently pushes the upper part of the seam toward the needle at a faster rate than the lower part. With a little practice it becomes easy to judge the easing accurately by eye and create perfectly eased seams.

When the thread in the bobbin runs low the bobbin must turn faster, and with less thread to damp the vibrations it makes a faint jingling sound. Sounds like this are usually not noticed until the user is intimately familiar with the machine. Then they become clues which the operator can interpret, allowing him or her to make more efficient use of the machine. Whenever I hear the bobbin's faint jingle, I check the thread level before starting a new seam. Thus I usually avoid running out of thread in the middle of the seam. Industrial sewing machines have separate bobbin winders which can wind one bobbin while a second is sewing. To wind bobbins, I leave about a foot of thread extending from the hole on the side of the bobbin and hang it over the edge of the table, using a small spring clamp as a weight on the end of the thread. This clamp frees me from further attention to the bobbin winder, as it eliminates the necessity of holding the end of the thread on the first row of windings. I hang the spring clamp on the end of a long thong attached to the bobbin winder, so it is always convenient. This method of winding bobbins requires two tubes of the same type of thread. If you have only one tube of thread, which is threaded on the machine, it is still possible to wind a bobbin without completely unthreading the machine. Simply unthread the needle leaving the thread in the lower thread guide, then remove the empty bobbin and transfer it to the winder. Then raise the presser foot (using the lever rather than the treadle or knee lift), thread the bobbin, and attach the spring clamp. Hold the thread loosely in front of the thread guide and the bobbin winder as you guide the thread onto the bobbin, and keep your left hand loose and springy. The sewing machine should never be operated without material between the presser foot and feed dog, as both of these parts can become damaged by such operation. Thus it is extremely important to make sure that the presser foot is raised when winding bobbins from a threaded machine in this manner.

To cover the subject of sewing machines completely here is impossible. Therefore I have only outlined the important aspects of the subject. The best way to learn to use a sewing machine is, naturally, by trial and error, through using your own machine. Every machine is slightly different. Some of the things I've mentioned may not even apply to your particular machine, but they should serve as good general guides for efficient sewing. In time, the characteristic jingles, rattles and clicks on your machine will become familiar to you, allowing

you to eliminate problems before they occur, so that your sewing will go smoothly and you will be relaxed. Remember — when she hums, she hums.

Most of the seams used in sewing leather are the same that are used in cloth. There are a few special seams which are unique to leather sewing. They either reinforce the structural stitching (taped seams), add to the visual effect (inverted seams), or simplify construction (simple lap seams). Many people who have never tried it believe that leather is more difficult to sew than cloth. Fortunately for leatherworkers, this is not the case. Because of its tendency to ravel when it is cut, cloth must have all of its edges bound, overcast, or turned under. However, since the fiber structure of leather is totally random, its cut edges do not ravel. Because of its directional weave, cloth must be cut perfectly, according to the grain. Again, the random fiber structure of leather eliminates this problem; it is only necessary to avoid unusually stretchy parts of the hide or else to cut them so that they work with the design (stretchy parts can be used very advantageously as pockets, for instance). Finally, leather doesn't require the extensive preliminary pressing and basting which must be executed before sewing cloth. To be sure, until a person becomes a very skillful sewer, some basting may be desired for accuracy around corners and curves. Accordingly, a stapler may be used to baste leather almost effortlessly. In certain instances glue is used for basting. Unless the basting must bear quite a bit of stress before it is sewn together (e.g., simple lap seams on curved seams tend to pull apart when being sewn), plain rubber cement can be used. Rubber cement is thinner and easier to use than shoe cement. Shoe cement gums up the needle; it should only be used when extra holding strength is required.

There are six basic considerations in deciding what method of construction to use for a certain application: strength, stitch durability, bulk, visual appeal, ease of construction, and ease of repair.

Strength is the most important factor I consider. Leather is in itself a strong material. But the durability of the finished piece is only as great as the strength of its weakest element —

art is wearing a hat and coat and carrying raveling bag, all made of garment cowhide

129

the seams. Ideally, the thread used for structural seams should be as strong as the material to be sewn. Any less than this will defeat the characteristic of graceful aging inherent in leather, and the seam will have to be resewn when it comes apart. Silk thread is beautiful but it isn't strong enough to withstand extensive stress and abrasion. Nylon thread is the strongest. It also has enough give to allow it to flow with the stress on the seam. Nylon thread comes in many sizes, colors and finishes. The usual sizes are 46 or 69 for lightweight garment leathers, 99 for bags and all-around sewing, and heavier weights such as 107 or 128 for heavy-duty work. If the number of the thread is preceded by a B it indicates that the fibers are bonded to keep the thread from raveling. Bonded threads tend to be rather stiff. An S indicates a soft finish that looks a lot like silk. S99 nylon as been my favorite thread for several years. Nylon is fusible, which makes it suitable for fused tie-offs.

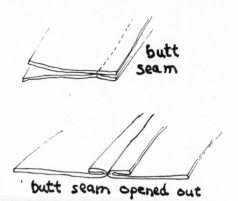

butt seam

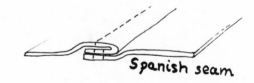

butt seam opened out

The structural stitching which I have mentioned is the plain butt seam. This seam can be glued open, double topstitched, or reinforced in various ways. The butt seam is the preliminary step to every other seam except the lap seam, which is not reinforced. Reinforcing butt seams reduces the stress on the structural stitching. The simplest reinforcement is the Spanish seam. (The terminology used here is only relevant between the covers of this book. Every tailor seems to have his own name for this seam: French seam, Spanish seam, Russian seam, side seam, single topstitch.) To make a Spanish seam the seam allowances of the structural stitching are both folded to one side and stitched down from the top surface. You will notice when you try this seam that it forms a ridge that varies in height according to how the material is manipulated. If the top surfaces are held taut, the ridge will shift to the backside of the material. This weakens the seam considerably as it puts the structural stitching in a position of higher stress. Properly done (the seam allowances pulled taut along with the rearmost layer of material), the ridge is shifted to the top, a strong position. The structural stitching should not be seen when the finished seam is viewed straight on. The seam allowances are

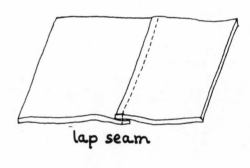

lap seam

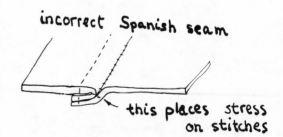

Spanish seam

incorrect Spanish seam

this places stress on stitches

folded over from the back *while sewing the seam*. This is standard procedure in all reinforced seams; folding and taping is done while sewing and it is often done blind, that is, from the back by feel. Excess seam allowance may be trimmed from the finished seam to reduce bulk and create a neater-looking backside. Trimming can be done very efficiently by sliding the shears rather than snipping with them. To do this, a small starting cut is required, and the shears must be held firmly with the points open only about ⅛ inch. If care is taken so that the points don't separate, the seam allowances can be safely trimmed extremely close to the stitching without cutting the threads.

This makes a very neat backside; but I must remind you about one of the original six considerations so that you will understand the shortcomings of this method as well. You will remember that I mentioned ease of repair. Exposed topstitching is occasionally subjected to a considerable amount of abrasion — enough to wear out the thread (even nylon) after a few years of constant hard use. Ordinarily, resewing these worn-out stitches should be quite simple, merely a matter of putting the needle through the original stitching holes. A closely trimmed seam, however, tends to pop out from under the presser foot so that the needle will not catch up the bottom layers of material. In areas of high abrasion (such as the inside seam of a trouser leg and the side seam on a jacket or vest), I do not trim the seam as closely. Sometimes I don't trim the seams at all.

A more elaborate seam is the flat-felled or French lap seam. It is very strong, attractive, and fairly compact. Although the topstitching is subject to abrasion, restitching is easily done in the event that the threads wear out. As might be expected, it is a difficult seam to sew but it is worth the effort. Flat-felled seams insure permanence in a garment. To make a French lap seam, first sew the structural seam with the right sides together using a ⅝-inch seam allowance. This places the seam allowance on the inside of the garment. Trim the upper seam allowance to ⅛ inch, then spread a thin coat of light rubber cement on the lower seam allowance and fold it over to meet the trimmed allowance. Open out the seam and, from the top, stitch down the finished seam allowances with a double row of stitches. Flat-felled seams are too bulky to be suitable for tight curves.

  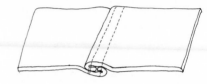

French lap seam (a)   French lap seam (b)   French lap seam (c)

Another very strong seam is the taped seam. Three versions of this seam are possible, each providing a different decorative effect. Two are sewn with the wrong sides together, thus placing the seam allowances on the outside of the garment. These are reinforced with tape cut from either the same or contrasting material. The tape should be cut about ½ inch wider than the open seam allowances.

For the first version, glue open the seam and align the tape over the open seam allowances. This works best with narrow seam allowances (³⁄₁₆-inch maximum); if the pattern uses wider seam allowances they should be cut down before gluing the seam open. The tape should be cut wider than necessary and trimmed after it is sewn on. The stitching lines should fall just outside the edges of the open seam allowances.

The second version involves applying the tape from the back. The tape is glued over the seam first, then the seam allowances are sewn down through all three layers with a double row of stitching. With the excess seam allowance trimmed close to the stitching, it is a neat, fanciful seam showing a contrasting strip of the leather's reverse side. I doubt that

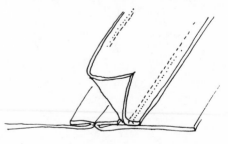

stitch on dashed lines
trim on dotted lines

Taped seam

stitch on dashed lines
trim on dotted lines

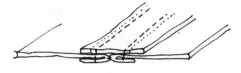

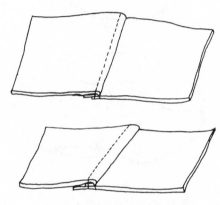

Trimming taped seam

Layering a Spanish seam

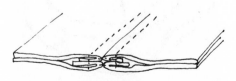

Two double-topstitched seams
back to back

this seam will ever gain a great deal of popularity, but it is interesting.

The third taped seam possibility is made with the structural seam sewn right sides together (the seam allowances face the inside of the garment). The structural seam is glued open and the tape is sewn on "blind," stitching from the inside of the garment while aligning the tape over the open seam behind the material (on the outside of the garment) by feel. The material is then turned over and the tape trimmed close to the stitching. This is a concise, practical seam with a very clean appearance. The tape can either match or contrast with the basic material.

Let's pause and compare all these seams, using my original six considerations:

Strength. Of the seams I've described, the French lap seam is the strongest because it has three rows of strengthening stitches. Spanish and taped seams have two rows and the simple lap, glued, and double-topstitched structural seams have only one.

Stitch durability. Resistance to abrasion is determined by two factors: the amount of exposure of the stitches and seam bulk at the stitch line. Less exposure and fewer layers of material at the stitch line mean greater durability. The seams from greatest to least durability, then, are as follows: plain structural seam glued open, simple lap seam, simple double-topstitched seam, the first of the three taped seams, the Spanish seam, the other two taped seams, and French lap seam.

Bulk. Although bulk is a factor in durability of stitches, its most important effect is on the line and body of the garment. When two seams are sewn face to face or when a seam is folded back upon itself, the resulting bulkier seam is awkward to sew and tends to dominate the shape of the piece. Sometimes layering is necessary to avoid sudden increases of bulk. All taped seams are layered in this manner. Spanish seams can be layered by trimming one seam allowance close to the stitching line and gluing down the untrimmed seam allowance. Where two double-topstitched seams are placed back to back, one of the seams may be trimmed and the other left untrimmed. The leather itself can also be skived down at the seam allowances. On soft leathers this can be done by laying a pair of shears with the blades open flat on the material of the seam allowance. Keeping the shears flat against the surface, close the blades carefully. Trim and taper to as narrow a width as possible the ends of seams which are to be turned or sewn into other seams. Around tight curves, seams must be clipped and notched to achieve a good shape.

Seam bulk gives body to the construction. This is a positive aspect and should be used to its best advantage. Seam allowance bulk on curved seams creates internal shaping stresses. An illustration of the usefulness of this characteristic is the body in hat brims. Several people I know put wire edges on their hat brims for shape. Without the wire, the brims are floppy and shapeless. I have found that utilizing the opposing stresses of a curved seam makes wire unnecessary and results in evenly distributed body and more natural shaping of the brim. Another example of manipulating seam rigidity to distribute body is Tom Tisdell's use of two side seams rather than one back seam on the crown of his western-style hats. This helps to keep the crown from squashing down. It should also be noted that Tom uses Spanish seams for this hat. Spanish seams are more rigid than the simple double-topstitched seams. On my fedora-style hat I control the shape of the brim by making two side seams on the top piece and one back seam on the bottom piece. This creates firm body all around the back of the brim, while allowing a slight natural droop in the front.

Visual appeal. Each seam has its own way of emphasizing the lines of a particular piece. The choice of which seam to use is a matter of personal taste and should be made to complement the piece you are making. Experience with all of the seams will make it easier for the designer to choose the seam which will correspond most closely with his own interpretation of the piece at hand.

Ease of construction. The Spanish seam is by far the simplest. After the structural seam is sewn only one more oper-

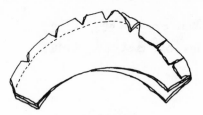

Notch or clip seams on curves

Use of side seams to create supporting stress

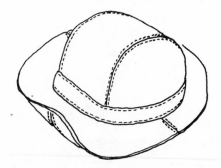

Even distribution of seams to create shape

ation is required. Gluing a seam open is more time-consuming, requiring two additional operations: spreading the glue and pressing the seam. True, pressing the seam need not take long if a good roller is used, but applying the glue neatly requires patience and precision. Double topstitching likewise requires two operations: a row of stitches up one side of the seam and another row back down the other side. French lap seams require patience: trim, glue, press, sew up one side and back down the other side — five operations. Taped seams can be complicated: glue, press, sew up one side, sew down the other side, trim one side, then trim the other side. Simple lap seams are not too hard, just glue and stitch. Unfortunately, this seam turns out to be most useful in areas which are extraordinarily difficult to begin with.

Ease of repair. There seems to be a slight correlation between difficulty of construction and ease of repair. Generally speaking, the more time you put into making a seam, the less time it will require in repairs. Restitching should always be done from the same side and in the same holes as the original stitches. This, however, becomes nearly impossible when the seam allowances have been trimmed too close to the stitching in the back of the seam (as sometimes happens with simple double-topstitched seams and Spanish seams). For this reason I rarely trim seam allowances to less than ⅛ inch from the stitching line, except in areas of zero stress or where control of bulk is crucial (e.g., the end of a seam that is to be sewn into a seam allowance). There is another problem which may occur in repairing reinforced seams. If the structural stitching gives way before the worn reinforcing stitches have been repaired, the reinforcing stitches will have to be opened up a few inches in either direction in order to do the repair by machine. This is laborious, as each stitch must be picked out individually, but it must be done in order to position the presser foot for sewing. On short breaks a second alternative becomes practical, which is to resew the seam by hand. In some cases (e.g., the French lap seam), the structural stitching is relatively unimportant and may be eliminated or ignored when doing repairs. Glued seam allowances also make repairs difficult. This demonstrates one reason for using a light rubber cement for gluing garments instead of using a super bond shoe cement.

Neatly made bound buttonholes quickly establish your reputation as a skillful garment maker. They are not hard to make and are by far the strongest buttonholes possible. To make bound buttonholes you need a welt pattern 1 inch longer and 1 inch wider than the buttonhole outline and a negative pattern through which slash lines may be stenciled onto the garment. The two may be combined in one template by cutting the slash lines from the center of the welt pattern, or the slash lines may be cut in their proper positions on the garment pattern itself for greater accuracy in successive efforts with the same pattern. A standard buttonhole ½ x 1 inch requires a welt pattern 1½ x 2 inches. Because the outline of the welts tends to show through on the surface of the garment with age, one edge of the welt pattern may be rounded or truncated to create a smoother appearance for more mellow aging. Slash lines should be cut with a very sharp pointed knife (such as the #11 X-Acto blade); always cut from the corners inward to avoid overshooting the corners. The small triangular tabs are then glued back on the reverse side of the garment and stitching lines are marked between the corner points. Glue is applied to the long tabs on the right side of the garment and the welts are laid directly on the glue right side down. The welts are then stitched from the back along the marked lines. The stitching must not extend past the corner points or it will cause bad puckering on the finished buttonhole. Glue is applied to the long tabs and the corresponding areas across the stitching lines. Each welt is pulled through to the back of the garment and pressed down, while the extending part of the welt is held taut so that the long tab folds precisely at the stitching line. Glue is applied to the welts, which are folded back so that they meet precisely at the center of the buttonhole. Accurate centering is very important to the appearance

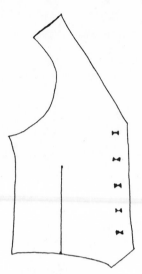

Slash lines for buttonholes on pattern

Rounding one edge of welt pattern

136

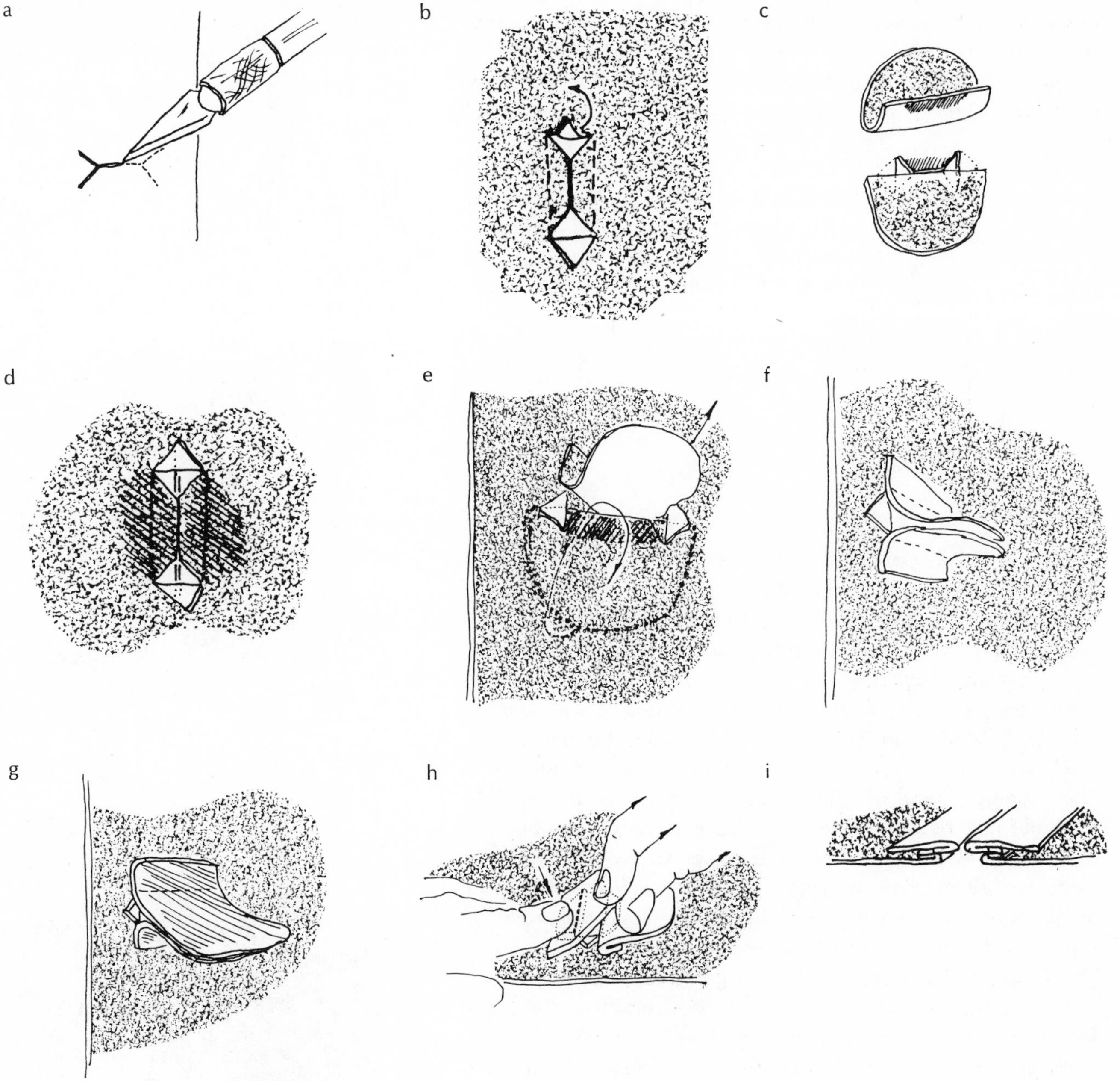

a

b

c

d

e

f

g

h

i

of the finished buttonhole. To reinforce the buttonhole, a row of stitching is sewn around it close to the edge. Buttonholes are generally set in the direction of stress, as this is the strongest position. If set in an opposing direction, the welts tend

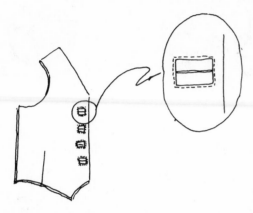

to pull out of shape. The only exceptions are in areas of very low stress (such as the front of a loose-fitting deerskin shirt), where the buttonhole positioning may be used to emphasize the design of the garment. Most buttonholes will be backed by a facing — the front edges of coats and vests as well as waistbands on pants and fitted jackets are almost always faced. After the facing is in its final position it must be slashed directly behind the buttonholes to allow for button insertion. The slashing should be made slightly longer than the buttonhole and may be done with an X-Acto knife, using the buttonhole as a guide. Great care must be taken to avoid nicking the welts and, again, the cutting should start at each side and meet at the center, to insure sharp corners. The final treatment of the slashed facing is not elaborate; the slash lines are simply glued back as far as they will easily go, glue is applied to the extending material of the welts, and the buttonhole and the facing are pressed together. Facings have their own peculiar construction techniques; I will go into more detail about them later. Buttonholes not backed by facings (such as those on pocket flaps) may be trimmed close to the stitching. When

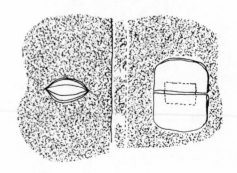

facings are used, leave the extending material of the welts in order to taper the bulk at the edge of the buttonhole (see Drawing i on page 137).

Once you know the technique for buttonholes, the transition to welt pockets is a logical (and simple) development. The pattern is essentially the same, but larger and with extended welt sections. To make a pocket pattern, simply draw an outline of the pocket as you would like it, then add a 1-inch border around it. Mark slash lines at the top of the pocket

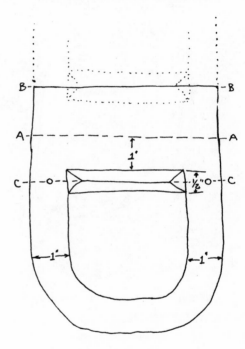

Welt pocket pattern

outline for ½-to-¾-inch-wide pocket opening. Now double the pattern at line AA. Cut the doubled pattern in two at line BB. The long part will be the upper welt and the small part the lower welt. With the slash lines cut out, the longer pattern can be used as a template for positioning and marking the pocket. The longer pattern can also be used for marking the small lower welt with CC as the cutting line, thus avoiding the necessity of two separate patterns.

The construction procedure is the same as for the buttonholes, but after stitching around the edge of the pocket opening (as with the buttonhole on page 138) a thin line of glue is applied around the edges of the welts and the upper welt is folded so that it is superimposed over the lower welt. The

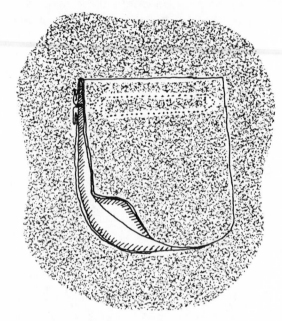

Folding the upper welt over the lower welt

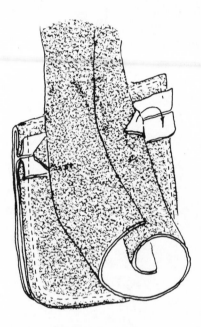

Sewing the pocket together

pocket is then sewn together by laying the garment right side up and pushing the material away to reveal the pocket, then stitching around the edges.

Slant pockets are only slightly more complicated. The pattern is again made by drawing an outline of the pocket as you want it, adding a 1-inch border, marking the slash lines, doubling the resultant pattern at AA (this creates a mirror-image effect), and cutting it in two at BB. For slant pockets, however, a seam allowance the width of the pocket opening must be added to each welt at BB in order to get the pocket to line up properly. These seam allowances are not merely extensions of the existing angles, but another set of mirror images. Notice the "windows" used for positioning the slash

Slant pocket pattern

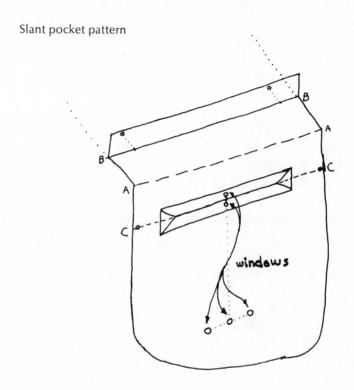

windows

lines. This particular pattern is the one I use for the upper pocket of a four-pocket fitted vest. The windows placed in a vertical line are positioned over the dart, which extends to the center of the upper pocket. The three holes in a row near the bottom are positioned over the lower pocket line. This system allows exact positioning of the pockets after the shape of the garment has been altered by darts, as is the case with the fitted vest.

As with straight pockets and buttonholes, the triangular tabs are glued to the back and the welts are glued to the remaining long tabs. Because of the angles, there is a discrepancy between the stitching lines and the edges, which necessitates the use of accurate alignment marks for positioning the welts on the long tabs of the pocket opening. You will notice that although the pocket pieces appear to be out of line, the pocket outline is positioned perfectly. This is the only difference in the construction of slant pockets.

Patch pockets are by far the easiest to make, and can be quite pleasing, especially when complemented with an attractive flap. Make the pattern with small fold-under allowances around the sides and bottom and a larger allowance along the top. This gives the pocket good shape-retaining qualities. The bottom of the pattern can be made curved, square, or with truncated corners. When making patch pockets, I glue the sides and bottom first, and when folding the allowances over, I fold the top corners about ⅛ inch farther in than the rest. This keeps them from jutting out when the top is folded down. While folding the edges, excess material around the curve (or at the truncated corners of square pockets) is pinched together so that small tabs are left sticking up from the folded-under allowance. The tabs should be evenly distributed for a smooth appearance in the final product. Press the fold with a seam roller, first one way, then the other, to insure flat edges. Then snip the tabs off with a pair of shears laid flat across the pocket. This is a good, precise way to notch any curved seam. Before sewing the pocket to the garment, sew around the top fold, or just along the top edge, if you prefer.

To sew the pocket to the garment, use a double row of stitches, widening into small triangles at the top corners to reinforce this area of high stress. An even more elegant treatment of these stress points, if it can be done neatly, is to make the extensions rounded rather than triangular. This eliminates practically the last vestige of stress. I generally sew the pocket on with the top edge humped up a bit, so it will be easier to reach into. For stretchy leathers, of course, this is unnecessary.

The flaps should be made slightly wider than the pocket.

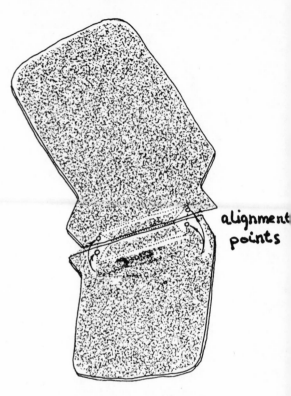

Positioning a slant pocket

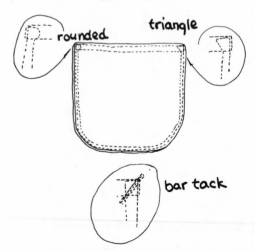

Pocket reinforcement styles

A buttonhole is always desirable on patch pocket flaps. I combine the stitching around the buttonhole with the edge stitching, which is done from one top corner to the other and around the bottom of the flap, leaving the top edge unstitched. When I reach the buttonhole I simply sew around it in a loop-the-loop. The threads are tied off at the corners and the buttonhole trimmed close to the stitching. There is no stress on

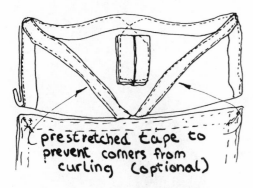

Attaching tape to pocket

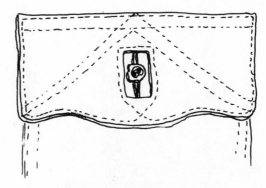

Attaching pocket flap to garment

the edges of the flap, so a single row of stitches is sufficient. To sew the flap to the garment, however, a double row of stitches must be used. I have found that patch pocket flaps offer a particularly good opportunity for creativity. Sometimes I dispense with a pattern altogether and simply fold the edge of a piece of leather the width I feel would suit the garment. It is interesting to make flaps out of leather with appropriately shaped natural edges (such as the leg portions of a goat or deer skin), leaving the raw edges unfolded along the sides and bottom. There is no need to stick to a standardized form; garments with patch pockets surely benefit from the individuality given them by free-form flaps.

Facings require a special technique to achieve a smooth, finished look. The inner edge of the facing is glued and folded under, and stitched if desired. The facing is sewn to the garment, right sides together, and the seam allowance of the facing is trimmed as close as possible to the stitching. Glue is

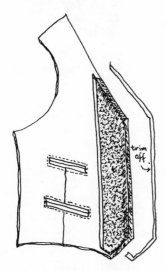

Attaching a facing

applied to the now-exposed right side of the other seam allowance and the corresponding area of the facing. This is pressed down *with the seam opened out*, pinching excess material at corners for notching. Done properly, this leaves a ridge right next to the seam line. Sharp angles are difficult with this procedure, but facings do not usually have to contend with sharp angles, and in any case the result is worth the trouble. Glue

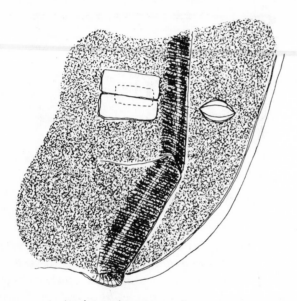

Applying glue to seam line

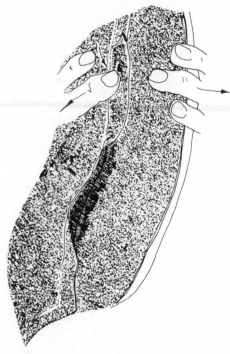

Pressing down edge of facing

is next applied to both sides of the seam line, and the facing and garment are turned right side out and pressed along the edges. If the pressing is done carefully, and all the preceding steps have been done properly, the seam line will be recessed about 1/16 inch. It is important to make this recess uniform and close to the edge. A neat appearance on the inside of the faced edge depends on your accuracy when topstitching along this edge. Stitching that slips in and out of the recessed seam looks awkward and will not do credit to your craftsmanship. The ridge you see just above creates the proper bulk for an even transition from the edge to the facing.

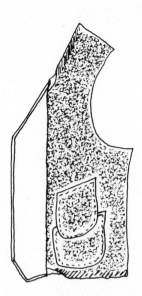

Recessed seam
line

Coats should always have full facings extending through the neckline. There is no suitable way to put in a coat collar without a facing. There are two methods for setting in collars. In the first method (used for better-fitted and heavier coats), the separate sides of the collar are sewn to the facing and the main portion of the garment respectively, between the seam allowances of the collar. The seams end at the stitching lines and do not cross onto the seam allowances. The seam allowances of the seams joining the collar sections, the neckline facing, and garment neckline are clipped to the stitching line at the ends of the seams and the seams are then double-topstitched. The full facing then includes a collar facing. This is sewn to the full garment and collar, the seam allowances cut close at corner points, and everything turned right side out. When everything is positioned properly, the edges are topstitched up one side, around the collar, and down the other side. Collar points are usually difficult to turn. The best tool for this is a good pair of needlenose pliers; it doesn't make it easy, but it makes it possible to turn practically any point, if it is done patiently. Rather than make a sharp pivot at collar points, I round them by two or three stitches. This is about as sharp a point as can be made with most leather, anyway.

With the second method, the two sides of the collar are sewn together, turned right side out, and stitched along the finished edges. Then the facing is sewn to the main portion of the garment, inserting the finished collar along the neckline. The front edges are then recessed as described earlier and stitched up one side, across the neckline, and down the other side. This method is the easier of the two. It is best suited to lighter jackets, as it produces a bulkier neckline than the first method. It also allows you to use self-facing patterns, in which only a short section of the neckline facing is cut separately.

The lower brims of double-brimmed hats are also variations of facings. There are two ways to sew a double brim. The first is to sew the brims to the crown and the sweatband respectively, using either Spanish or double-topstitched seams. Sew the brims together, inside out, notch the seam allowance heavily using a knife or a V-shaped punch, spread glue over the brims and turn them inside out. After smoothing all the lumps and evening out edges, the brims are sewn together around the edge. To get a good shape with this method requires a vegetable-tanned kip or other stiff leather; it is not suitable for garment leather. The second method starts out the same: the top brim is sewed to the crown, the bottom brim to the sweatband, and the two are stitched together with a narrow (⅜-inch) seam allowance. Next, the two sections of the hat are pulled apart and the seam around the edge of the brims is double-topstitched. This is a bit tricky until you get used to it, since the stitching is essentially done from inside the hat. Rather than sew two separate seams here, the two rows of stitching are sewed continuously, connected with a couple of stitches crossing the seam at the back (centered, of course). One or both seams are trimmed close to the stitching and strong glue is applied to the remaining seam allowances; when only one seam allowance has been trimmed, the other seam allowance must be glued down. When the glue is tacky, another application is spread entirely over the brims. The hat is then turned right side out — working quickly to avoid getting the brims stuck together in the wrong positions. Finally, the brims are pressed thoroughly with a seam roller or a rubber or smooth-faced wooden mallet. When only one of the seam allowances is trimmed, it creates a layered effect and gives more body to the brim than when both seams are trimmed. This type of brim can be made with any type of light leather with excellent results, and it is actually less time-consuming than a notched brim, but it takes a good deal more skill to do it well (this should not discourage you from attempting this brim; it should encourage you to start practicing on it sooner).

Darts are merely incomplete seams used to improve the fit of garments in localized areas. The most critical part of the dart is the point. If it is sewed badly, it will form a "bubble," which comes from sudden rather than smooth, even tapering at the point. Most people find that it takes a lot of practice to make perfect darts, so don't get discouraged too easily. The easiest way to make darts is to cut a slit along the center line

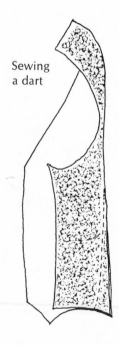

Sewing a dart

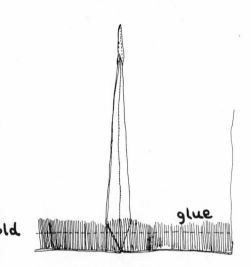

fold   glue

Tapering wide end of dart
before gluing

to within ½ inch of the point. Then fold the dart along this line, making sure that the edges of the slit are lined up well, and sew it with a slightly curved taper. By the time you reach the top of the slit, you should be less than ⅛ inch from the edge. Continue tapering until you are as close to the edge as you can get without falling off the material entirely, then continue straight for a few stitches more and tie off the thread. With practice it is possible to make the last stitches just through the flesh, not piercing the surface of the leather at all. Hammering the fold will help achieve this effect, as will the use of thinner needles. Because the tie-off at the point of a dart is exposed to constant abrasion, you may want to make a double knot. The edges of the dart should be glued down and the bulk at the point should be hammered flat. To eliminate bulk at hems and cross seams, the wide end of the dart should also be cut at an angle, before gluing.

The easiest way to insure a perfect fit on custom garments is to have the recipient of the garment try it on inside out with strategic seams (side and back seams, darts) left open. With a stapler it is a simple matter to take in the seams to the exact configuration of the body. Areas that are badly out of proportion can even be completely altered by adding darts or seams other than those in the pattern.

The easiest way to get a set of patterns is from the catalogs of the big pattern companies. The patterns may not fit as well as they're supposed to, but they are good starting points to work from, and alterations, as I've just explained, are not difficult. The tissue paper that commercial patterns are printed on is worthless if you are seriously planning to use the pattern more than once. Even if you do plan to use a pattern only once, it is a good idea to transfer the pattern to better material just for accuracy. The simplest material for patterns is smooth cardboard. Large sheets of poster board can be purchased inexpensively. Of course, the heavier the board, the more durable the pattern will be. Quarter-inch Masonite composition board is impervious to most abuse and has the added advantage that it can be used to hold the leather in place while cutting around the pattern. The necessity of marking the pattern outlines with grease pencils and tailor's soap is thus eliminated. Plexiglas is by far the best pattern material. Not only will it perform all the functions of the Masonite, its transparency allows you to see any imperfections in the leather before you begin cutting. If you can afford it, and you have the tools for cutting it to shape (such as a bandsaw), it will be worth the trouble to make Plexiglas patterns for your favorite tested patterns.

Most of the examples I have given in this section have been for hats and vests. I have had the opportunity to make hundreds of hats — over twenty different styles. Each style has had its unique problems as well as problems common to other styles. Because hats require only a small material investment and incorporate such a variety of techniques (not to mention their salability), they make ideal practice projects for developing skill in working with garment leathers. Vests are useful projects for developing skills used for fitted garments. When constructing the vest, make the darts, pocket, buttonholes and facings first. Then sew the side seams. (On custom vests the back and side seams may be basted temporarily to adjust the fit on the individual. A stapler is excellent for this basting step.) At this point glue down the hem allowance of the armhole curve (armscye). Clip along the curve every inch or so, leaving about 2 inches at the top of the curve open to facilitate sewing the shoulder seam. After sewing the shoulder seam, glue down the remaining hem allowance and stitch one row around the armscye. Now sew the two sections of the vest together at the back seam. Once the two sections are joined, all that remains is gluing and stitching around the edges of the vest and sewing on buttons. With this method you are always working with the smallest possible portion of the vest, thus avoiding awkward handling of larger portions. Anyone with this basic background should have no problem tackling more advanced projects.

Although I have devoted quite a bit of time to sewing machine techniques, there are occasions when hand stitching is preferable. Many hand stitches are impossible to achieve with a machine. Sewing machines can do the constant tedious work of stitch after stitch, but they can never put on the finishing touches that tell of true craftsmanship. If you are not impatient, the simple repetition of hand sewing can be very relaxing.

There are five basic stitches for hand sewing: the running stitch, the saddle stitch, the whip stitch, the buttonhole stitch, and the cross stitch. More elaborate stitches such as the herringbone stitch may also be used. Except for saddle stitching, in which needles are fastened to each end of an armspan length of thread with bleed knots, hand sewing needles should always be threaded double. Double threading not only eliminates the need for knotting, it is also twice as strong in the final product.

Whatever you do, try to remember that the object is to relax and have a good time, and to make sure that everything you do is done with love.

List of Suppliers
and
Bibliography

List of Suppliers

Beacon Leather Company, 106 South Street, Boston, Massachusetts 02111.

Beacon has all kinds of shoe findings, hand tools, hardware, finishes, and a modest line of nice side leathers, bends, etc. If you look around the back of the shop, you may find some bargains in used tools.

Berman Leather Company, 147 South Street, Boston, Massachusetts 02111.

Berman has a large selection of side leathers, shoulders, bellies, butts, and bends as well as some deerskins, elkhides, cabrettas, etc. It also has a large supply of buckles, finishes, hardware, cut soles, and some hand tools.

Capitol Shoe Findings, 117 Beach Street, Boston, Massachusetts 02111.

Capitol has the best selection of used tools including skiving machines, sole cutters, shoe anvils, etc. They occasionally have shoe lasts and hat blocks when they can get them.

Century Leather Company, 110 Beach Street, Boston, Massachusetts 02111.

Century has garment leathers, calfskins, hair-on pony hides, sheepskins, and kidskins. Century is the only place that I know of that has had cordovan shell horse. It also has a complete line of finishes and some buckles.

Charrette, 2000 Massachusetts Avenue, Cambridge, Massachusetts 02140;
139 East 47th Street, New York, New York 10017.

Charrette has architects' and designers' supplies. For $5 it will send you a 20 percent cash discount card and a complete catalog.

Elton Leather Corporation, 47–49 Spring Street, Gloversville, New York 12078.

Elton has high quality deer, elk, moose, hair sheep, and pig skins. Some odd lots are available at bargain prices.

M. Siegel Company, 186 South Street, Boston, Massachusetts 02111.

"Siegel's" has the best selection of all types of leather. It also has an extensive line of tools, hardware, and finishes, as well as the most complete assortment of buckles. Write to them for leather swatches and their catalogue of tools and buckles.

Tandy Leather Company, 8117 Highway 80 West, Fort Worth, Texas 76116.

Tandy has branches everywhere. Write for their catalog.

Bibliography

Ashley, Clifford W. *The Ashley Book of Knots*. Garden City, N.Y.: Doubleday & Co., 1944.

Grant, Bruce. *Encyclopedia of Rawhide and Leather Braiding*. Cambridge, Md.: Cornell Maritime Press, 1972.

Hollen, Norma R. *Flat Pattern Methods,* 2nd ed. Minneapolis: Burgess Publishing Co., 1965.

Newman, Thelma R. *Leather as Art and Craft*. New York: Crown Publishers, 1973.

Papanek, Victor. *Design for the Real World*. New York: Pantheon, 1972; Bantam, 1973.

Tanous, Helen Nichol. *Designing Dress Patterns,* 3rd ed. Peoria, Ill.: C. A. Bennet Co., 1971.

Vogue Patterns. The "Everything About Sewing" Series. New York: Butterick Fashion Marketing Co.

Wanneh, Gawaso (pseud. for Arthur C. Parker). *The Indian How Book*. New York: George H. Doran Co. Available at the Museum of Natural History, New York City.

Waterer, John William. *Leather Craftsmanship*. New York: Praeger, 1968.

Whife, Archibald. *A First Course in Gentlemen's Garment Cutting,* rev. ed. London: Tailor & Cutter, 1968.

White, George M. *Craft Manual of North American Indian Footwear*. George M. White, P.O. Box 365, Ronan, Montana 59864.

Wilcox, R. Turner. *The Mode in Footwear*. New York: Charles Scribner's, 1948.

Willcox, Donald. *Modern Leather Design*. New York: Watson-Guptill Publications/Ballantine Books, 1969.

Willcox, Donald, and Manning, Jim. *Leather*. Chicago: Henry Regnery Co., 1973.

Wilson, Eunice. *A History of Shoe Fashions*. New York: Theatre Arts Books, 1969.

Wright, Thomas. *Romance of the Shoe*. Detroit: Singing Tree, division of Gale Research Co., 1969 (reproduction of 1922 ed.).

In addition to this brief list, there are many books on costume design and historical costume development that have useful information and drawings of various stylized garments and accessories. Even more valuable are the numerous volumes of folk legends and fairy tales with illustrations depicting elaborate and ingenious outfits. The illustrations of Howard Pyle are particularly important. Books on aboriginal (Indian) cultures may also contain helpful information and illustrations.

Craft Horizons, the magazine of the American Crafts Council, 44 West 53rd Street, New York, New York 10019, contains valuable stimuli for contemporary craftspeople.

Patterns

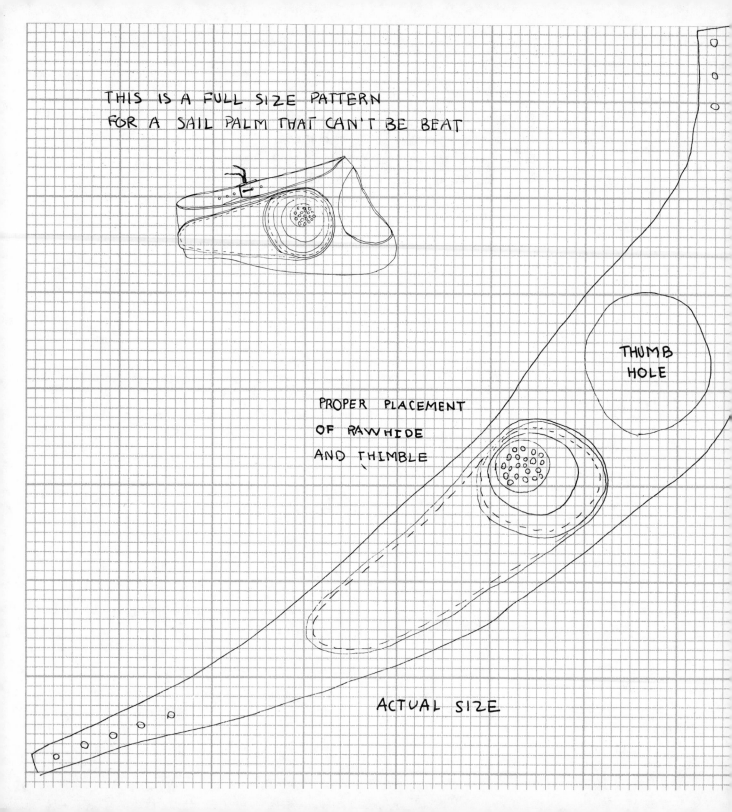

THIS IS A FULL SIZE PATTERN
FOR A SAIL PALM THAT CAN'T BE BEAT

PROPER PLACEMENT
OF RAWHIDE
AND THIMBLE

THUMB
HOLE

ACTUAL SIZE

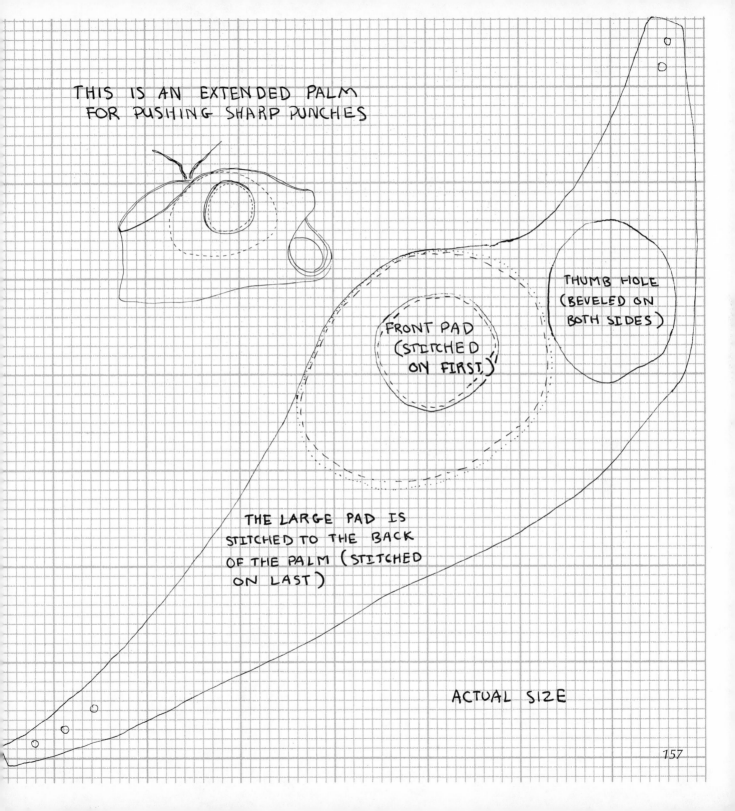

THIS IS AN EXTENDED PALM
FOR PUSHING SHARP PUNCHES

THUMB HOLE
(BEVELED ON
BOTH SIDES)

FRONT PAD
(STITCHED
ON FIRST)

THE LARGE PAD IS
STITCHED TO THE BACK
OF THE PALM (STITCHED
ON LAST)

ACTUAL SIZE

157

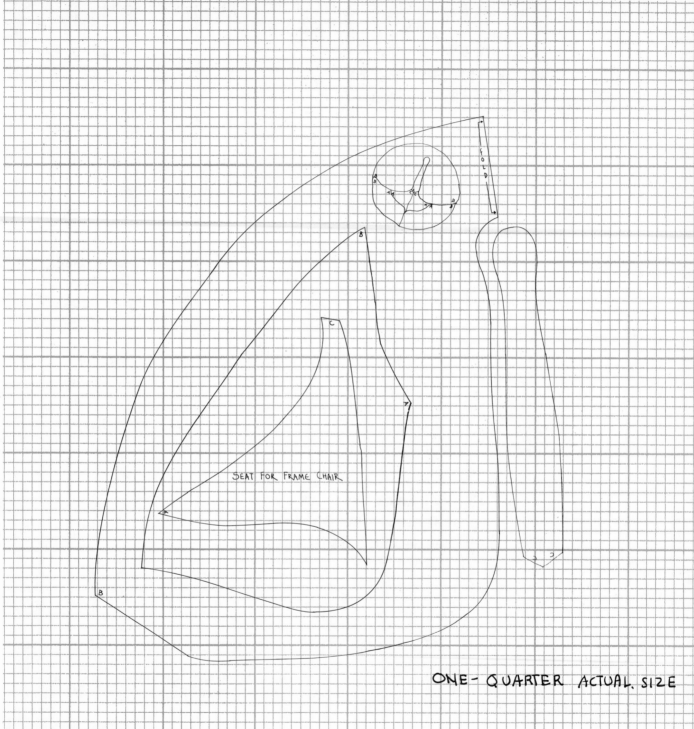

SEAT FOR FRAME CHAIR

ONE - QUARTER ACTUAL SIZE

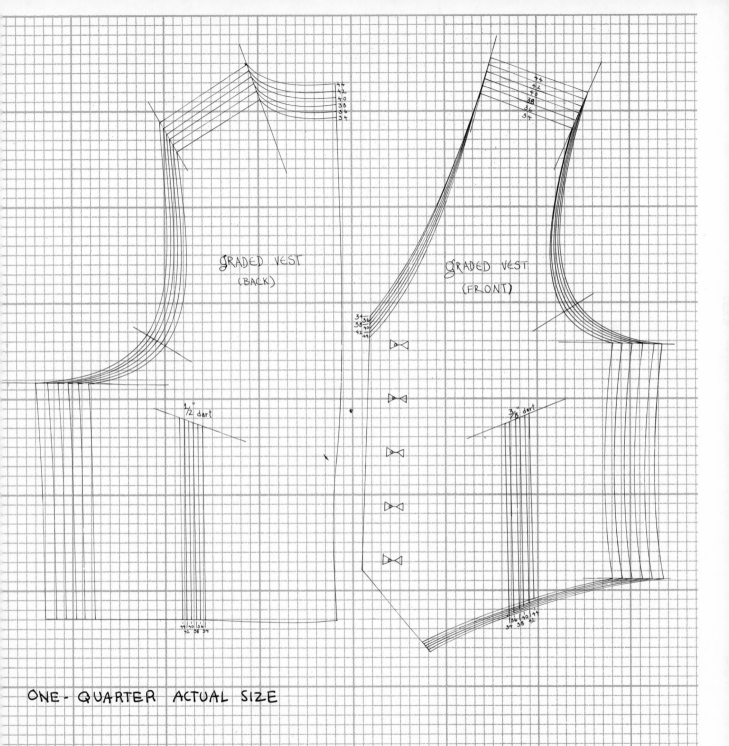

GRADED VEST
(BACK)

GRADED VEST
(FRONT)

1/2" dart

3/8" dart

ONE-QUARTER ACTUAL SIZE

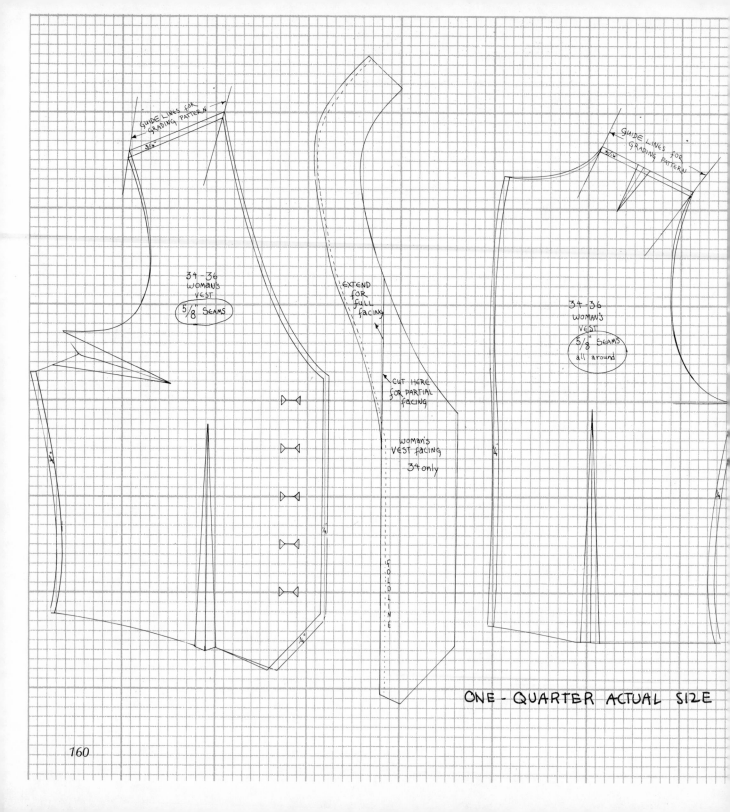

GUIDE LINES FOR GRADING PATTERN

3/4"

34-36 WOMAN'S VEST

5/8" SEAMS

EXTEND FOR FULL FACING

CUT HERE FOR PARTIAL FACING

WOMAN'S VEST FACING 34 only

FOLD LINE

GUIDE LINES FOR GRADING PATTERN

3/4"

34-36 WOMAN'S VEST

5/8" SEAMS all around

1/4"

1/4"

3/8"

1/4"

3/8"

ONE-QUARTER ACTUAL SIZE

160

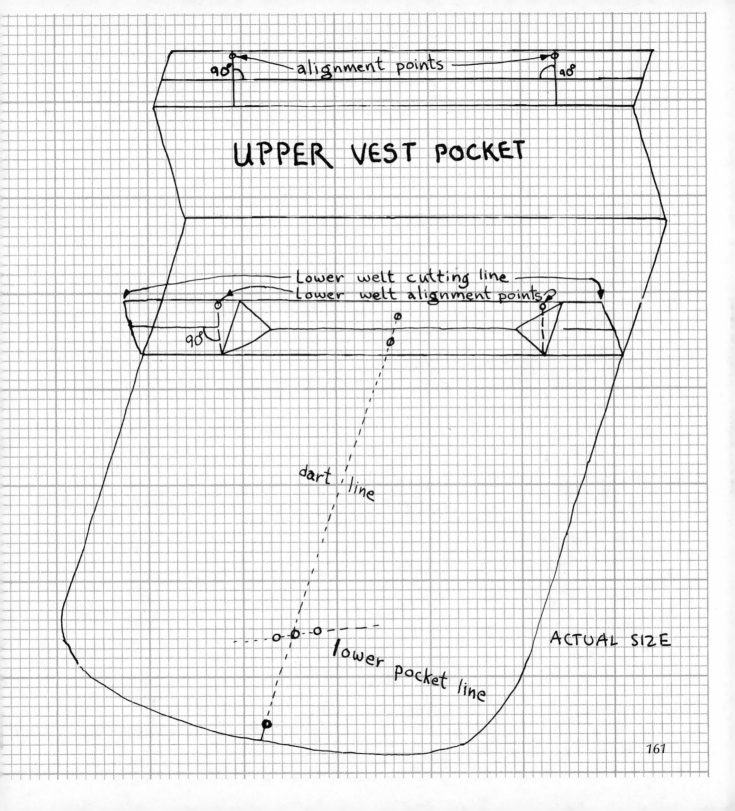

UPPER VEST POCKET

alignment points

90°   90°

lower welt cutting line
lower welt alignment points

90°

dart line

lower pocket line

ACTUAL SIZE

161

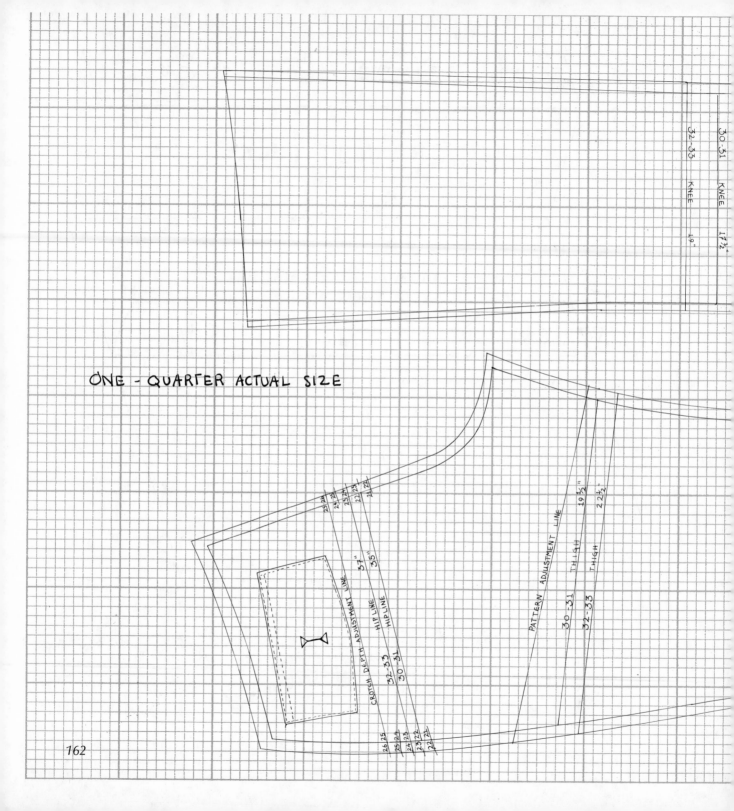

ONE - QUARTER ACTUAL SIZE

30-31 KNEE 17½"

32-33 KNEE 19"

CROTCH DEPTH ADJUSTMENT LINE

HIP LINE 37"

HIP LINE 35"

32-33

30-31

25 25

25 25

23 23

22 22

21 22

26 25

25 24

24 23

23 22

22 21

PATTERN ADJUSTMENT LINE

30-31 THIGH 19½"

32-33 THIGH 22½"

162

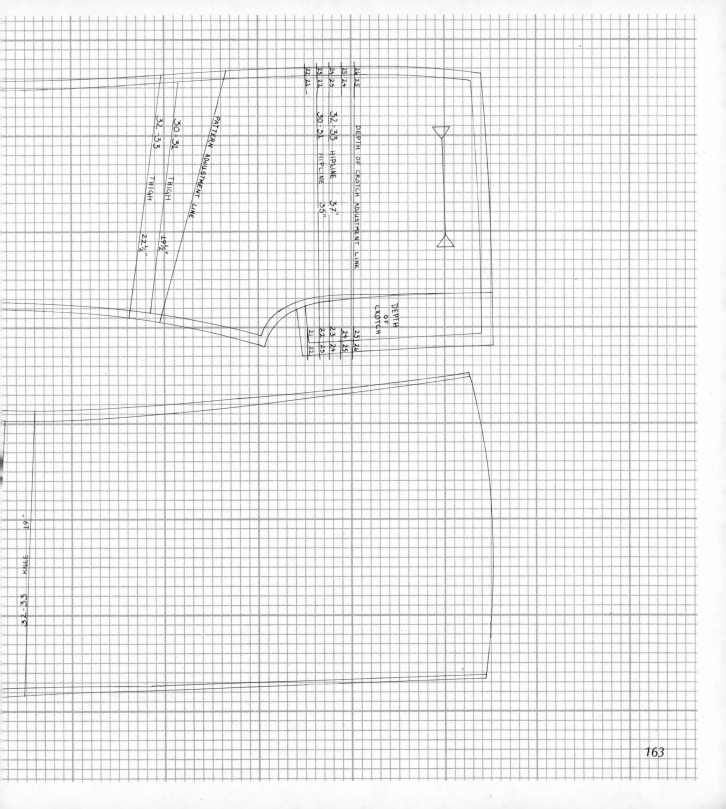

DEPTH OF CROTCH ADJUSTMENT LINE

26 25
25 24
24 23 · 32-33 · HIPLINE 37"
23 22 · 30-31 · HIPLINE 35"
22 21

32-33 · THIGH 22½"
30-31 · THIGH 19½"

PATTERN ADJUSTMENT LINE

DEPTH
OF
CROTCH

25 26
24 25
23 24
22 23
21 22

KNEE 19"
32-33

163

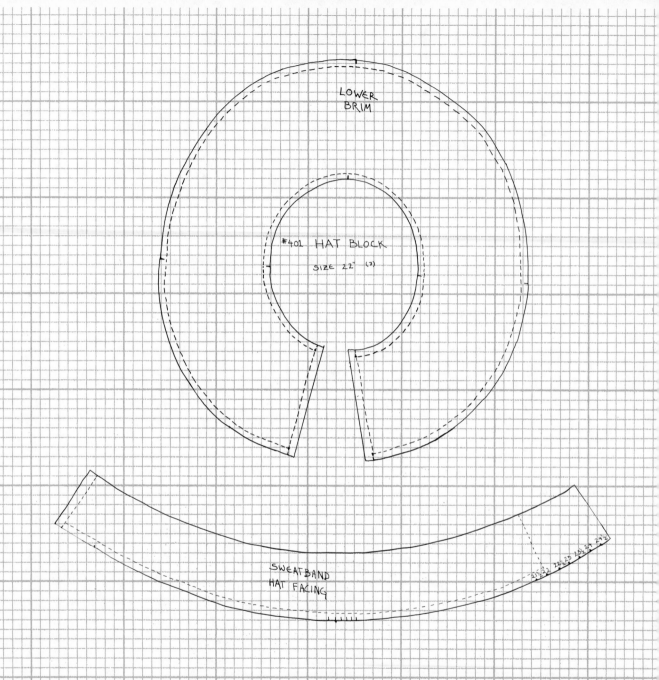

LOWER
BRIM

#401 HAT BLOCK
SIZE 22" (7)

SWEATBAND
HAT FACING

ONE- QUARTER ACTUAL SIZE

164

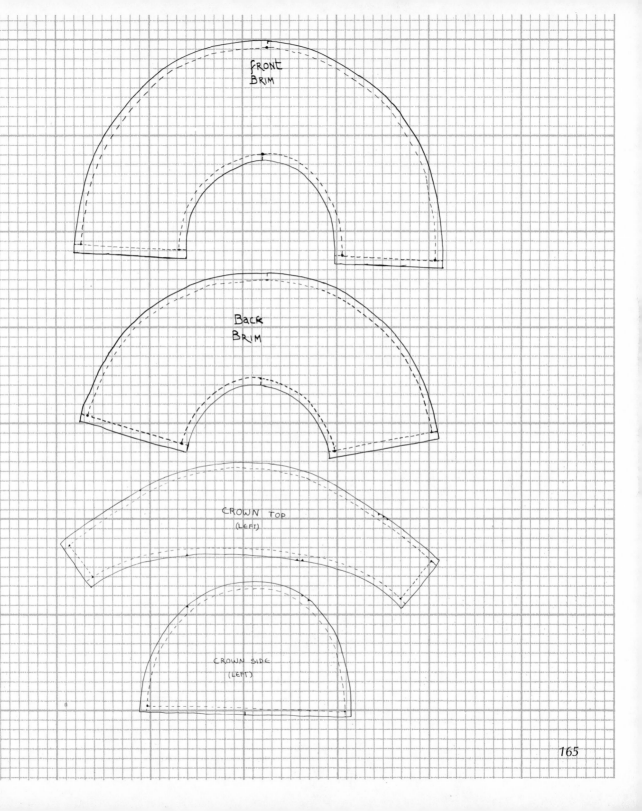

FRONT
BRIM

BACK
BRIM

CROWN TOP
(LEFT)

CROWN SIDE
(LEFT)

165

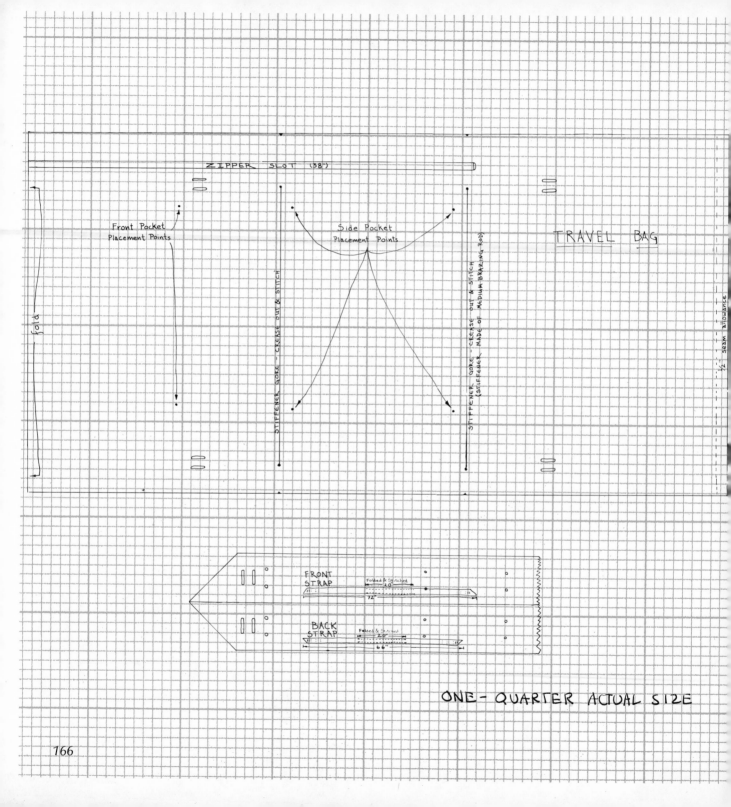

ZIPPER SLOT (38")

Front Pocket
Placement Points

Side Pocket
Placement Points

TRAVEL BAG

fold

STIFFENER GORE – CREASE OUT & STITCH

STIFFENER GORE – CREASE OUT & STITCH
(STIFFENER MADE OF MEDIUM BRAZING ROD)

½" seam allowance

FRONT
STRAP

Folded & Stitched
20"

72"

BACK
STRAP

Folded & Stitched
20"

66"

ONE-QUARTER ACTUAL SIZE

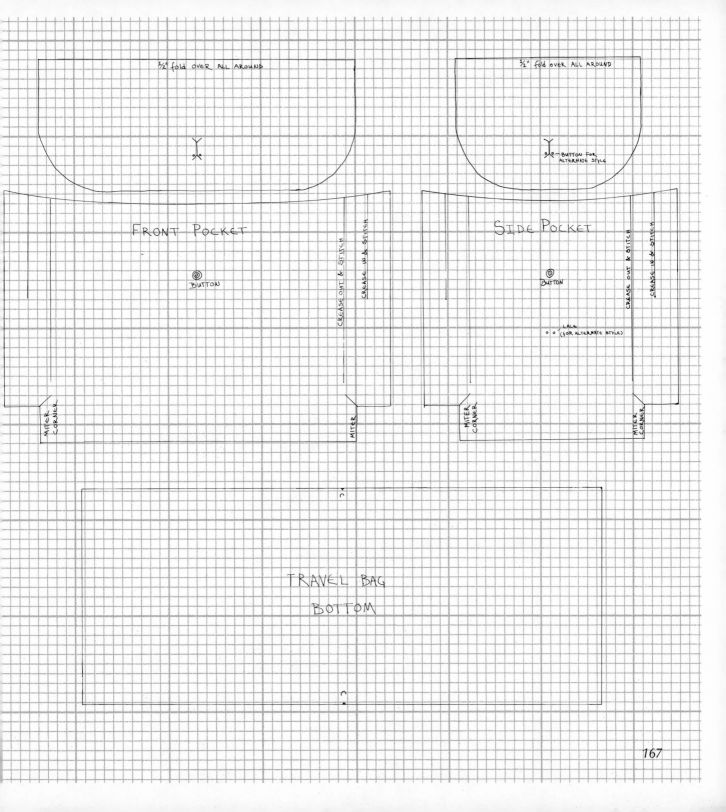

½" fold over all around

½" fold over all around

— BUTTON FOR
ALTERNATE STYLE

FRONT POCKET

SIDE POCKET

CREASE OUT & STITCH

CREASE IN & STITCH

CREASE OUT & STITCH

CREASE IN & STITCH

BUTTON

BUTTON

LACE
(FOR ALTERNATE STYLE)

MITER CORNER

MITER

MITER CORNER

MITER CORNER

TRAVEL BAG

BOTTOM

167

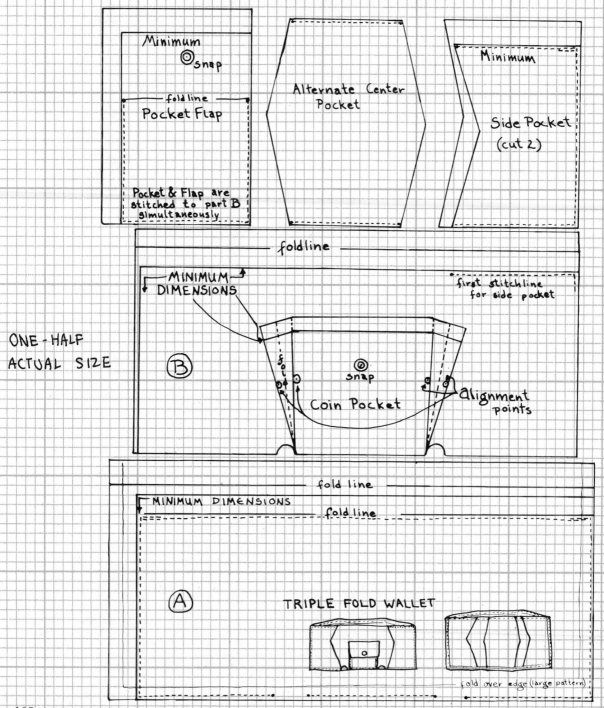

Minimum

snap

fold line
Pocket Flap

Pocket & Flap are
stitched to part B
simultaneously

Alternate Center
Pocket

Minimum

Side Pocket
(cut 2)

foldline

MINIMUM
DIMENSIONS

first stitchline
for side pocket

ONE-HALF
ACTUAL SIZE

B

snap

Coin Pocket

Alignment
points

fold line

MINIMUM DIMENSIONS

fold line

A

TRIPLE FOLD WALLET

fold over edge (large pattern)

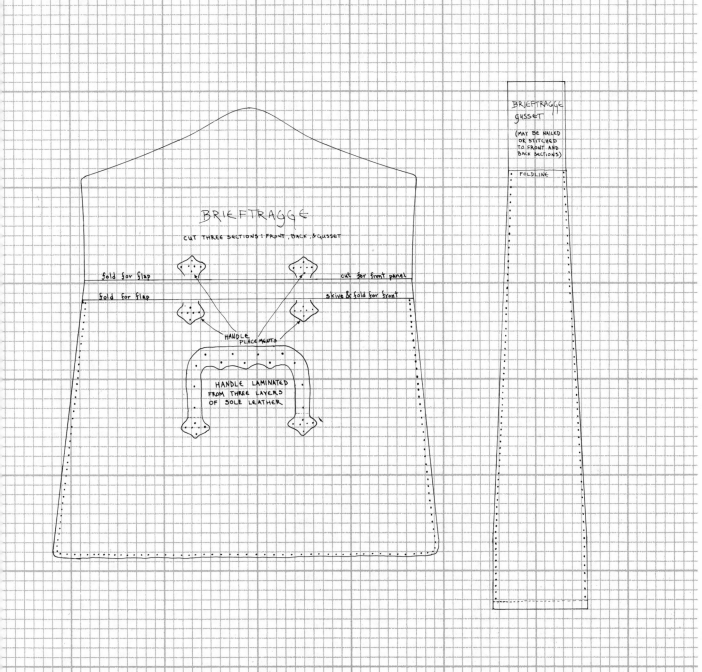

BRIEFTRAGGE

CUT THREE SECTIONS: FRONT, BACK, & GUSSET

fold for flap   cut for front panel

fold for flap   skive & fold for front

HANDLE PLACEMENTS

HANDLE LAMINATED
FROM THREE LAYERS
OF SOLE LEATHER

BRIEFTRAGGE GUSSET

(MAY BE NAILED
OR STITCHED
TO FRONT AND
BACK SECTIONS)

FOLDLINE

ONE - QUARTER ACTUAL SIZE

169

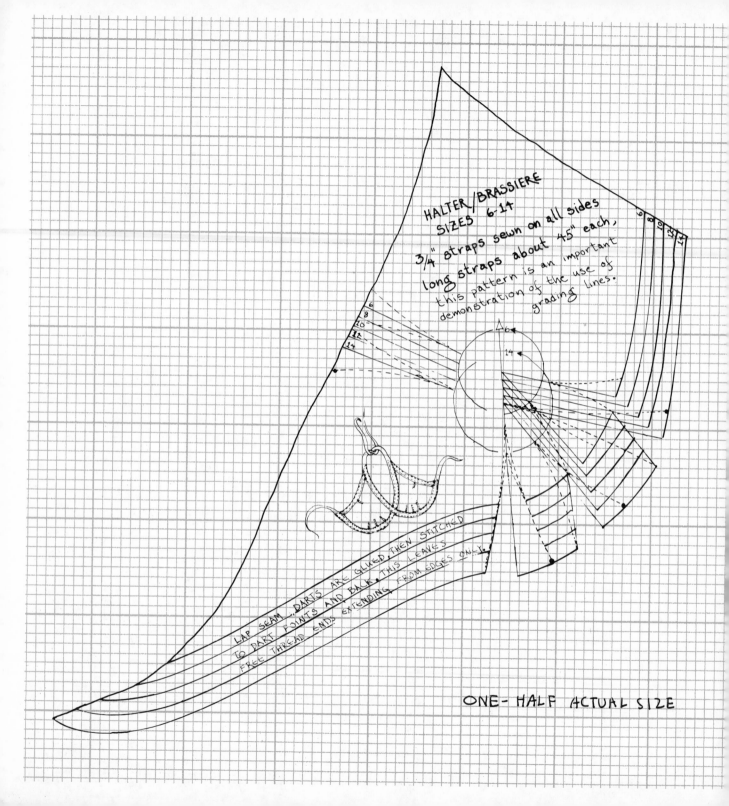

HALTER/BRASSIERE
SIZES 6-14

3/4" straps sewn on all sides
long straps about 45" each,
this pattern is an important
demonstration of the use of
grading lines.

LAP SEAM. DARTS ARE GLUED, THEN STITCHED
TO DART POINTS AND BACK. THIS LEAVES
FREE THREAD ENDS EXTENDING FROM EDGES ONLY.

ONE- HALF ACTUAL SIZE

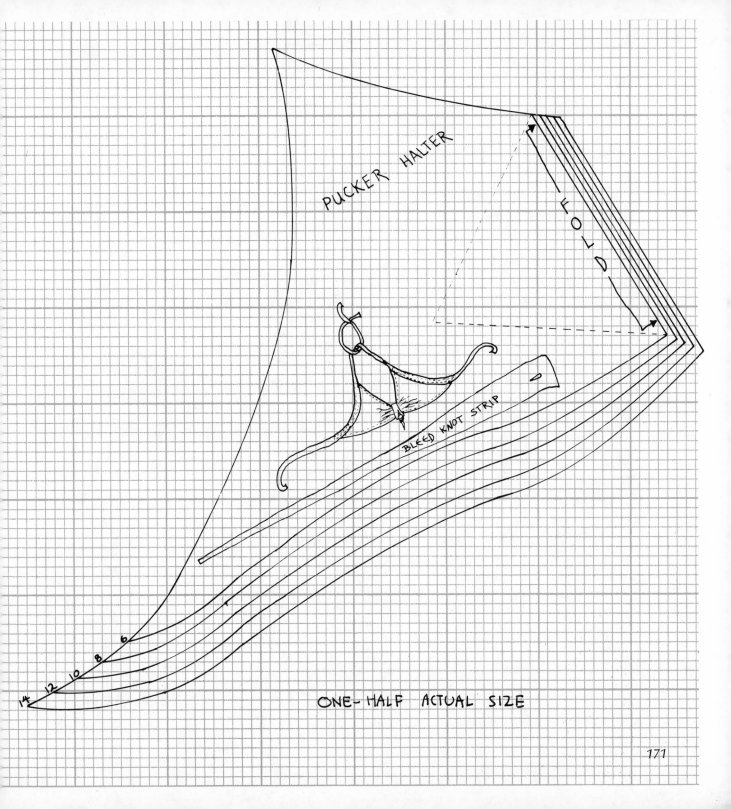

PUCKER HALTER

FOLD

BLEED KNOT STRIP

6
8
10
12
14

ONE-HALF ACTUAL SIZE

171

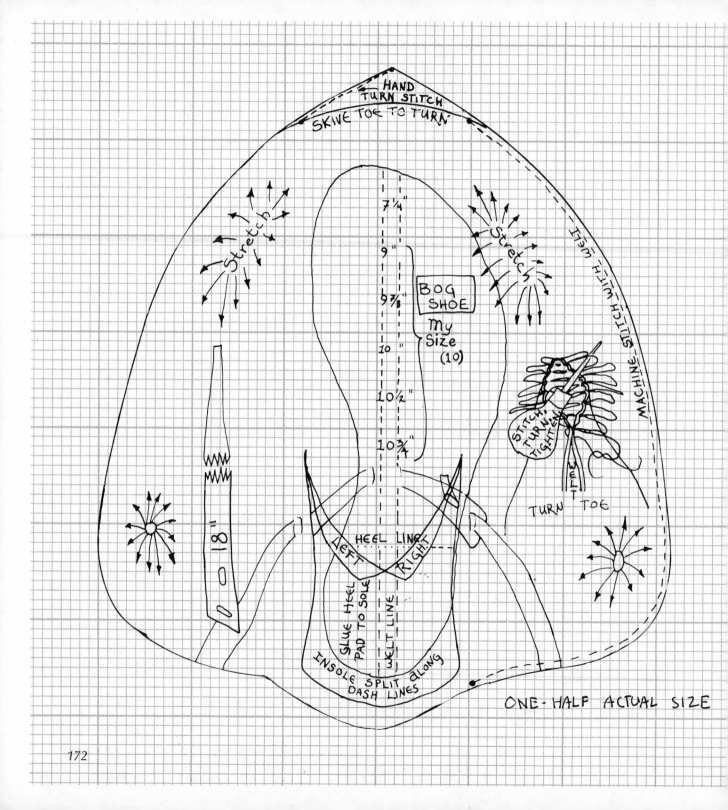

ONE-HALF ACTUAL SIZE

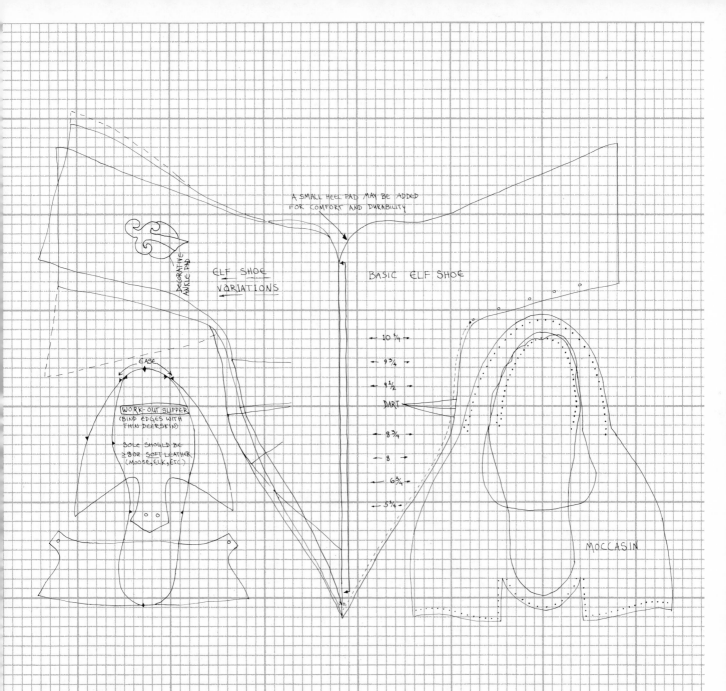

A SMALL HEEL PAD MAY BE ADDED
FOR COMFORT AND DURABILITY

DECORATIVE ANKLE PAD

ELF SHOE
VARIATIONS

BASIC ELF SHOE

EASE

WORK-OUT SLIPPER
(BIND EDGES WITH
THIN DEERSKIN)

SOLE SHOULD BE
≥ 8 OZ SOFT LEATHER
(MOOSE, ELK, ETC.)

← 10¼ →
← 9¾ →
← 9½ →

DART

← 8¾ →
← 8 →
← 6¾ →
← 5¼ →

MOCCASIN

ONE-QUARTER ACTUAL SIZE

173

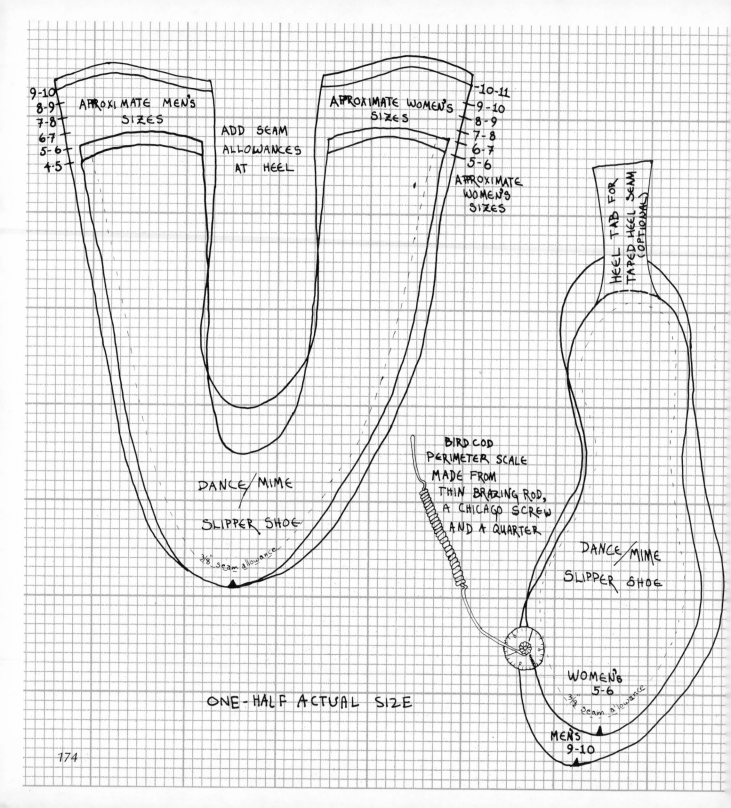

9-10
8-9
7-8
6-7
5-6
4-5

APPROXIMATE MEN'S
SIZES

ADD SEAM
ALLOWANCES
AT HEEL

10-11
9-10
8-9
7-8
6-7
5-6

APPROXIMATE WOMEN'S
SIZES

APPROXIMATE
WOMEN'S
SIZES

HEEL TAB FOR
TAPED HEEL SEAM
(OPTIONAL)

DANCE/MIME

SLIPPER SHOE

3/8" seam allowance

BIRD COD
PERIMETER SCALE
MADE FROM
THIN BRAZING ROD,
A CHICAGO SCREW
AND A QUARTER

DANCE/MIME

SLIPPER SHOE

ONE-HALF ACTUAL SIZE

WOMEN'S
5-6

3/8"
seam allowance

MEN'S
9-10

174

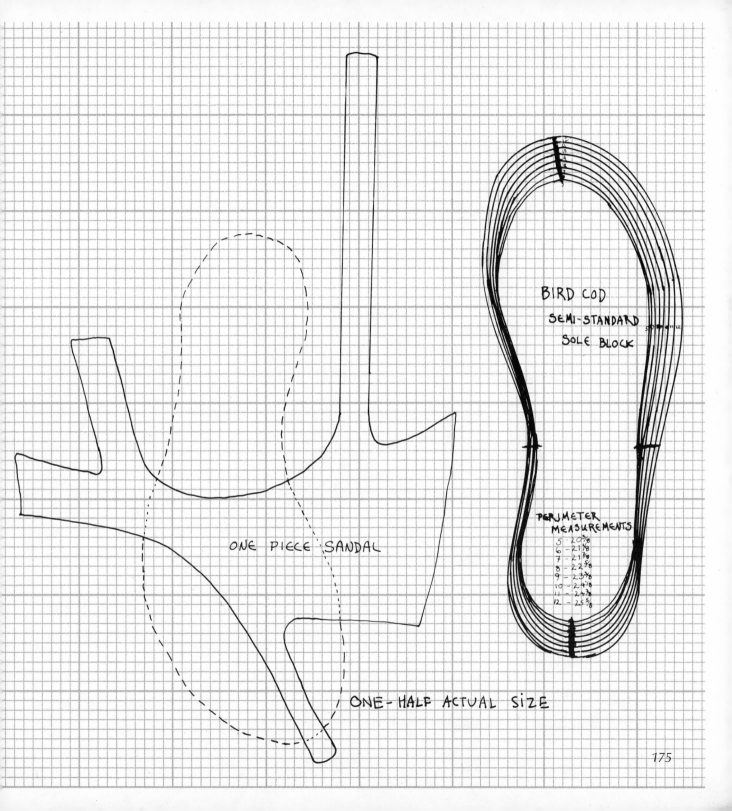

ONE PIECE SANDAL

ONE-HALF ACTUAL SIZE

BIRD COD

SEMI-STANDARD

SOLE BLOCK

PERIMETER
MEASUREMENTS
5 - 20 3/8
6 - 21 1/8
7 - 21 7/8
8 - 22 5/8
9 - 23 3/8
10 - 24 1/8
11 - 24 7/8
12 - 25 5/8

175

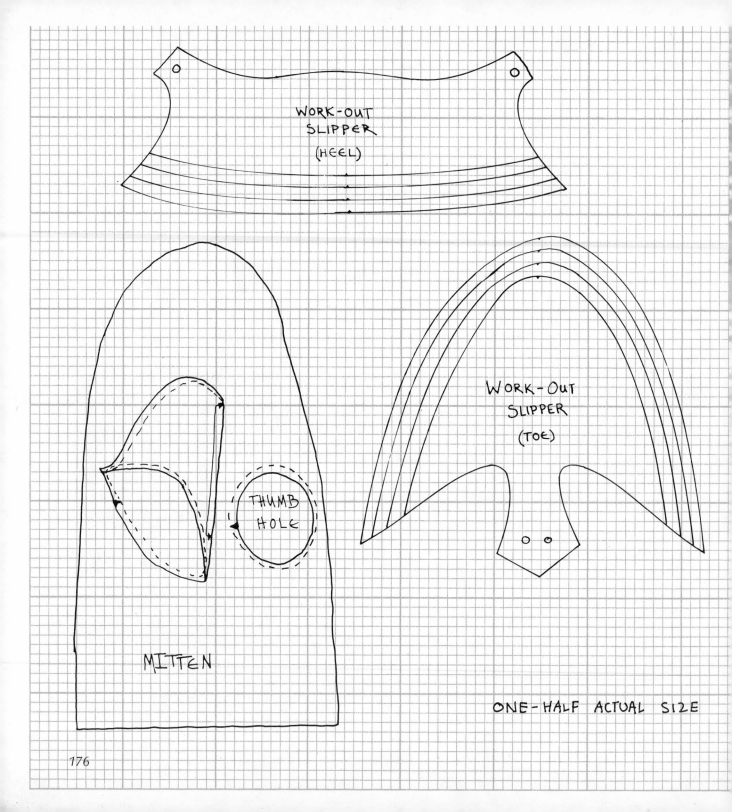

WORK-OUT
SLIPPER
(HEEL)

WORK-OUT
SLIPPER
(TOE)

THUMB
HOLE

MITTEN

ONE-HALF ACTUAL SIZE

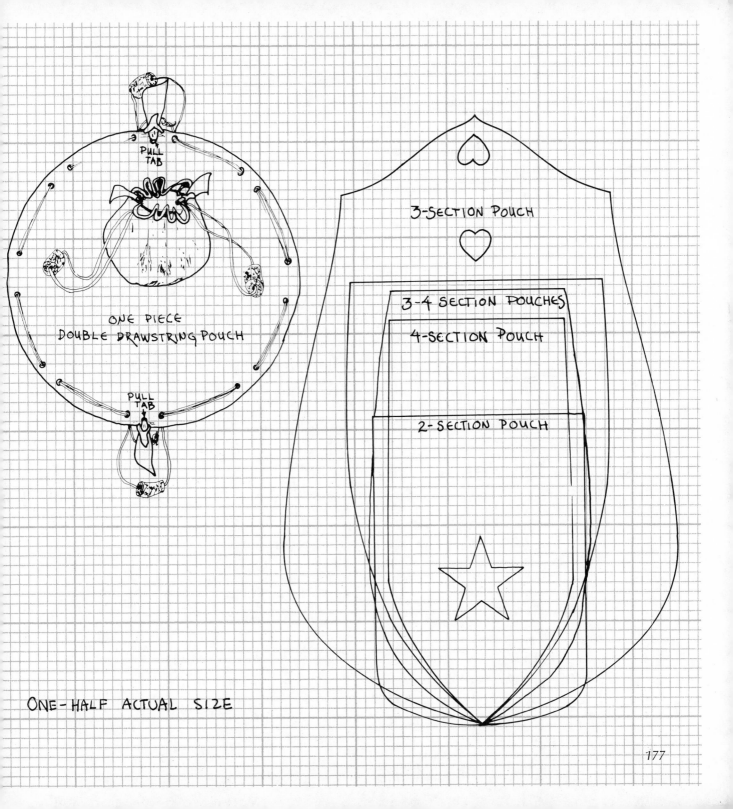

PULL
TAB

ONE PIECE
DOUBLE DRAWSTRING POUCH

PULL
TAB

ONE-HALF ACTUAL SIZE

3-SECTION POUCH

3-4 SECTION POUCHES

4-SECTION POUCH

2-SECTION POUCH

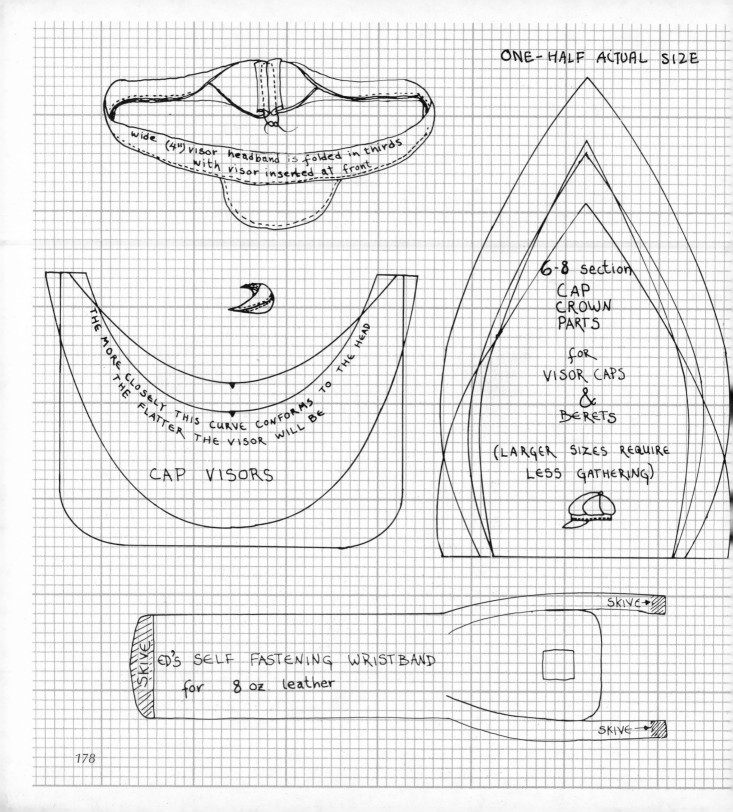

ONE-HALF ACTUAL SIZE

wide (4") visor headband is folded in thirds
with visor inserted at front

6-8 section
CAP
CROWN
PARTS

for

VISOR CAPS
&
BERETS

(LARGER SIZES REQUIRE
LESS GATHERING)

THE MORE CLOSELY THIS CURVE CONFORMS TO THE HEAD
THE FLATTER THE VISOR WILL BE

CAP VISORS

SKIVE→

SKIVE

ED'S SELF FASTENING WRISTBAND
for 8 oz. leather

SKIVE→

178